HELLO, Dr.Wells

Ann Dunham

ISBN: 1-4392-4096-5
ISBN-13: 9781439240960

Visit www.booksurge.com to order additional copies.

Dedication

Steve, Jeff & Jana

Grandma Patsy & Grandpa Ron

Grandpa Wayne & Grandma Ruth

Grandma Kathy & Grandpa LeRoy

Uncle Wayne, aka Whatface!

Uncle Mark, who is with Jesus

Cousin David

Acknowledgements

Numerous individuals have walked alongside Sarah in order to grant greater understanding, and along the way they have offered many individual considerations speaking to a resounding and singular theme—spending time with Sarah is a gift that grows unique insight into life, thus expanding the age-old notion that the "least of these" also teach us much. Thank you to all who have given so much while helping Sarah. A heart felt thank you to Barbara Dowling, Doctor Lloyd A. Wells, and Bret and Marie Merkle.

Forward

Upon the autism diagnosis, it seemed important to remember everything about Sarah's journey. I am not a doctor. I am not an educator. I am a mother, who has also been a constant observer. This book chronicles experiences related to autism and psychosis as they relate to my family. *Hello Dr Wells* is necessary because my memory can no longer contain all the facts. The writings remain either purposeful or annoying to the many teachers, doctors and other professionals embarking upon Sarah's journey. Since she is such a mystery, the written history of both her learning and psychosis might offer some important perspectives to other readers. The primary purpose behind this endeavor is to inform those who want to understand Sarah. My writing style is not professional, as it jumps between actual experiences, reflections, and musings. This work contains some terminologies that are associated with life in the world of autism. My lack of formal education will be evident, but will not make the chronicle of Sarah any less important. Additionally, I do not mean to entertain or embellish, because her story is what it is. Upon setting out to make this available through a publisher, I told Sarah that her story might be important to some people. She has an important testimony. The story behind her story; is that of the sacrifice imparted by my other two children, Jeff and Jana. Their acceptance in sacrifice during Sarah's upbringing makes for a sweeter offering, *Hello Dr. Wells* being that offering.

Table of Contents

Chapter 1: In the Beginning

Sarah Ann
Who is she?
An angel. An imp. An angel, imp, chimp.
What is she?
Two. Golden brown curly locks. Her eyes look right past you.
Why is she?
Because she is joy, hope and love.
Where is she?
Sleeping soundly for now.
When is she?
Whenever she wants.
How is she?
Sad. Mad. Sometimes bad. But mostly glad.
(1993)

Hello, Dr. Wells

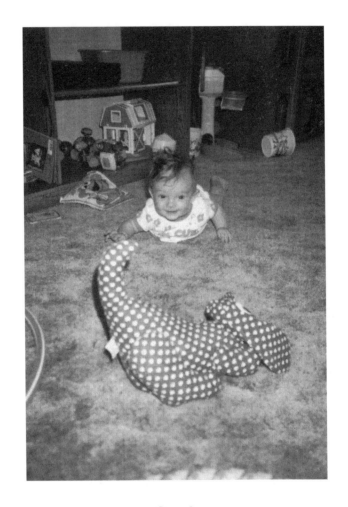

Sarah

Ann Dunham

From birth to diagnoses, 1992 through 1995. I conceived Sarah while heavily under the influence of Dr Seuss. My use of birth control hardly seemed to matter. The blessing of my first two, Jeff and Jana, came about with differing 99 percent effective methods. For me, birth control really represented birth in His control. After the doctor shared surprise number three, he concluded the visit by mentioning it might be a good idea to remove the IUD to prevent injury to the baby. A rather common pregnancy followed the IUD removal, except for the early and regular contractions; they confounded the doctor and happened with all three of my kids. While Sarah's delivery proved to be ordinary, her beauty was extraordinary. I had a living Precious Moments doll, one that could not keep her food down. As I awoke from a not so peaceful slumber in the hospital bed, the on call doctor mentioned Sarah's fussiness and inability to hold food down. Since Jeff and Jana were also very colicky as newborns and infants, I simply reassured the doctor that it was par for the course. That was that, and so Sarah came home after a very brief stay at the hospital.

She did not seem as colicky as Jeff and Jana had been. Since she was baby number three, I became accustomed with how to deal with a fussy baby. Yep, I considered myself an old pro at the whole thing. White noise, swings, blankets, bouncing, burping, bathing, barfing, barfing, barfing, and then came New Years Eve. Sarah did not hold anything down, and she became listless. I took her to an on call doctor first thing New Year's Day. Upon examining her, the doctor felt the need to look further and he ordered tests at a nearby hospital. An initial ultrasound indicated a possible problem, and a successive more reliable test resulted in the diagnoses of pyloric stenosis. Sarah had a defect that kept food from moving through the digestive tract properly, and that required surgery. Per the local hospital's instruction, we traveled about an hour down the road to Loma Linda for further care. Upon arrival, the Loma Linda doctors made skeptical statements about the diagnosis and asked us to leave her overnight. They actually insisted we leave and come back in the morning. I regretfully left, but my job was to remain with her; she was only three weeks old. The Loma Linda doctors confirmed the diagnoses, and surgery happened the next morning. Everything went well and soon enough Sarah was home again, eating incrementally better according to the feeding schedule the doctors gave us. She seemed alert, happy, and normal. Normal meaning, what I already experienced with her brother and sister, who were two very colicky infants.

As an infant, Sarah seemed indifferent and a bit defiant about being held, and it did not really bring her any comfort. But then again, when the other two were infants, being held did not soothe their colic either. Motion soothed all of them; they all liked motion, white noise, and distraction. Sarah moved her arms and legs constantly earning her the nickname of Going Nowhere Fast. She achieved milestones such as holding her head up, sitting up, crawling, and walking, earlier than most children. However, she did not pick up on speech in the same fashion as the other two. Jeff talked early and Jana talked quite a bit later than he did. Sarah did not show typical signs of language development, making her the latest talker by far. She did not seek out interaction and, at times, she was hard to engage. Her aloofness and the fact that we all tended to cater to this youngest child earned her another nickname, Queen Sarah.

Ann Dunham

Sarah

Hello, Dr. Wells

Sarah's first birthday came and went with little concern about her development. She met most of her milestones early, and even with her aloofness, she represented absolutely joy. It was not that she rejected us; she just seemed happier to be on her own. While she did not gravitate toward typical language development, as early as one year old we heard her imitate the evil queen's laugh from an animated movie. She also imitated Darla in a Little Rascals movie by saying, "No, no, no way." We made a game out of counting as Steve held up each finger, "One, two, three, four, five." We even made a game out of saying, "Daddy." While fully capable of repeating those words, she did not seem to equate their meaning; or if she did understand their meaning, she did not apply it. She seemed to utilize the words as a form of verbal stimulatory behavior, and not as a form of actual communication. Since every child's development is different, we hoped she just needed more time.

Many afternoons she played with her shadow for long periods of time. She loved getting into the silverware drawer and I had to scoot her away from it constantly. She played in the sand or water indefinitely if I let her. A friend, who helped me with her one day, felt Sarah was a genius because she played in the wading pool for over an hour, simply watching the water drip from her hands. Similarly, at the park she liked to throw colorful fall leaves and watch them float to the ground. In our yard, she sat and threw sand just to watch it fall over and over again. At the time of that preoccupation, we were desert rats and there was definitely lots of sand around!

Ann Dunham

Jeff and Sarah

Hello, Dr. Wells

I developed concern upon Sarah's second birthday, since she did not care about the gifts and did not even know what to do with them. She displayed total indifference, not even interested in unwrapping them. It seemed as if she just did not get it. I approached the pediatrician when she was a little over two, and foremost on my mind was the fact that she did not talk. He told me to be more imaginative and give her time. Obviously, I failed to give the doctor more specifics about the other things that she did. That might have resulted in a closer look. I did not know that the little things she displayed, and the bigger things that she had yet to display, indicated a hard fought life-long journey. Her characteristics at that time best described as non-verbal, somewhat anti-social, with increased involvement in self-stimulatory behavior. Was it that she was non-verbal or anti-verbal? She had the occasional ability to talk, but she very rarely did.

I kept busy with the kids, even homeschooling Jeff for kindergarten. Sarah would scoot, crawl, and then walk around, taking note of what was going on around her. Yes, she took it all in and she seemed to be an expert at doing so. She just seemed more interested in living life from the perspective of a spectator. I actually counted that as a blessing, thinking it evened up the score, especially when I considered the difficulties Jeff and Jana experienced due to their extreme and long bouts with colic. During this time, I had a preoccupation with a toxic tort to which we had signed, and that Erin Brockovich made popular. Jeff, Jana, and Sarah accompanied me on a seemingly infinite number of trips out to the area of contamination. We liked taking pictures and talking to folks who lived in the area; we even found ourselves occasionally speaking to some people who worked at the facility. The kids played amateur detective with me on those days. Other than that, we did all the typical things worth doing for young families. We lived on our little piece of heaven on an acre and a quarter of land. We did improvements around our house, made outings in the desert, and entertained friends.

We moved away from all we knew and loved since my husband, Steve accepted an offer to relocate and realize a promotion. In June of 1995, we made our move from the warm California desert to South Dakota;

a place where one loved one lamented, they do not even bury their dead in winter due to the cold, frozen ground. South Dakota seemed a far cry from the piece of heaven we occupied in the California desert. Still, we became thrilled with how Sarah handled the move. Her happiness thrived in the new house with two levels. She loved going downstairs by herself to chase her hand, play with her shadow, or watch an animated movie. Around this time she started to flap her hand just off to the side of her face, watching from the corner of her eye. When she did, it made people curious, and I found myself justifying the behavior by telling them that it seemed to give her comfort, and hands fascinated her.

One evening, later in the summer of 1995, we rented a movie in which the main character engaged in many of the same behaviors as Sarah. His condition did not have a good prognosis. I remember crying that night. Her issues overwhelmed me. On one hand, she had age appropriate large and small motor development. On the other hand, she definitely marched to the beat of a different drummer when it came to her communication and interaction. My brother had been a late talker, and it was often said that I, his younger sister by thirteen months, was responsible for teaching him to talk. We even had our own distinct baby language. Before I came along, he pointed and grunted to get what he wanted. He typified for me the representation of a child who developed at his own pace, and turned out fine. While he developed his skills in language, he prohibited my skills in walking by pushing me down every time I tried to walk, making me the fastest crawler alive. The point is, babies do adapt and grow according to their circumstance, no matter the circumstance. The problem with this point is that Sarah was not developing as everyone said she must.

My core responsibility remained that of providing a nurturing and fun environment for Sarah to develop at her own unique pace. Her oddities with communicative function might have always been there, only becoming painfully obvious when we could tangibly perceive what did not happen for her in speech and social interaction. Part of figuring the whole thing out encompassed the passing of time, and the evidence of skills not yet developed. I have always wondered how a

Hello, Dr. Wells

child can receive the diagnosis of autism at an age when milestones are not supposed to be evident yet. How can one possibly know, until the developmental stage has passed and the milestone missed? Even so, I waited maybe a bit too long to know Sarah's issue. Finally, in October of 1995, as she approached three years old, I attempted to get to the bottom of things and scheduled an appointment with a family practice doctor. The purpose of the visit was to have Sarah's hearing checked, even though she could hear bath water that was running upstairs, while she was downstairs. On the day of the visit, I told the doctor that she did not talk or seem to understand simple commands like: come here, let's go, and come and eat. The doctor asked if she experienced trauma, in any way. I told him she did not; we all catered to Sarah, and there was no explanation for her communicative delay. Sarah held the doctor's attention for quite some time as she danced about the room ignoring him. She refused any attention and hardly allowed for examination, so he scheduled a hearing test and made referral to a pediatrician.

Within a couple of weeks tests confirmed there was nothing wrong with Sarah's hearing, and the examination by a pediatric doctor resulted in referral to a developmental specialist. A long conversation with the doctor prepared me for the fact that Sarah was on her way to receiving a label of autism. The diagnosis spoke volumes and meant so very little, as far as an actual answer, and it seemed to rob us completely. While Jeff (six), Jana (four), Sarah, and I walked to the parking garage after the evaluations, Jeff asked why I was crying. I told him that Sarah might never talk. I called Steve when we got home, and I was barely able to speak through my crying as I told him about the doctor visit. He said rather forcefully and in his own descriptive narrative, not to worry, no doctor could tell that from one visit and there is nothing wrong with Sarah.

While we waited on the appointment with the developmental specialist, the local school district performed a free screening. During the screening the nurse mentioned that Temple Grandin, a well known high functioning autistic woman, was in town for a book signing. I went to that book signing and while there, I met Barb, an individual soon to play a significant role in unlocking the mystery of Sarah. I also picked up a couple books that shaped my approach in dealing with her development. Book smarts seemed to be the way to go, even though Sarah's life experience is a sort of learn-by-doing one. For Sarah, plug and play never works. While cramming on her issues, I anxiously awaited her visit to the specialist. I was still hoping it was all a mistake.

Sarah got a visit to the developmental specialist a little before her third birthday. In the later part of 1995, there came a morning filled with observations, questions, more questions, and the completion of questionnaires. A little after noon she received the label again, and for me that represented closure in the diagnostic process, not an answer. At any rate, the specialist provided therapy and placement options and wanted to meet again in another month. Sarah immediately started speech therapy, with placement in an early childhood program following shortly thereafter. I laughed as I walked Sarah into the preschool room on the first day, because the very woman I met at the book signing was Sarah's teacher. Barb was ready to be a part of Sarah's daily life.

(1/30/96) Classroom journal entry: Today was a much better day for Sarah. She has had a hard time separating from you, but that is normal for all children who spend quality time with mom... Today she quieted with the music box, but also enjoyed the dollhouse and a living book on the computer. Sarah does not comfort easily so I am allowing her to come on her own to the activities that we do. We "set up" things she enjoys and let her approach on her own. As she adjusts to her new surroundings and becomes more secure, we will ask for more "on demand" activities. She would come to the table and watch the other children, and even want to participate, especially if the activity involved a toy that had music or voice output on it. She did a wonderful job playing with the dollhouse. Nice play skills. She was even interested in the kitchen again today... She had juice today but did not eat a snack. (Barb)

Hello, Dr. Wells

During Sarah's first days in preschool, I learned about the importance of the teacher, and the role of the multidisciplinary team. The district multidisciplinary team observed, and evaluated Sarah. At the end of a forty-five day observational placement, the team presented the same label as the doctors, and then we all met to make it official. Most on the team moved on, once they offered suggestions on teaching via the Individual Education Plan (IEP). Documentation of Sarah's skill levels remained an important piece of the ever-growing puzzle. However, the only thing that bought the pieces into place was the teacher's ability, to put into practice the documented words and recommendations on the IEP. Without exception, Barb always backed up what she said or read with beneficial and properly applied interventions. With regard to the school experience, it really came down to one person. Barb drew from the enormity of her experiences through the years and uniquely applied techniques to give Sarah a chance. Chance, after all, happens to us all.

For some time to come, I experienced the weirdest kind of melancholy being the mother of such a puzzle, her autism associated with missing pieces. Many years needed to pass before I considered her whole, albeit a different kind of whole from my other two kids. Sarah did not require a lot of sleep and she engaged in motion constantly, and that required unwavering vigilance on our part. Some friends suggested that I lock Sarah in her room so I could get some rest. I did not want to do that because as tired as I felt, Sarah needed to be amongst us. I felt ongoing parallel interaction to be better than decreased interaction, because that provided a bigger chance of making a connection, finding an interest, or seeing a breakthrough. No lock on Sarah's door meant that, as I had just per chance gone to sleep in the wee hours, I would awake to find her cinnamon footprints throughout the house, or an ongoing pepper party in the kitchen. One of my all time favorites being the time that she poured an entire container of cocoa on our white couch. Why did we have a white couch anyway? The grand finale proved to be that of our infamous Sarah dancing outside, while running up and down the huge steps leading to our front door, in only her diaper, in thirty degree below zero weather with snow and ice on the ground. She joyfully laughed at the elements, and then laughed at the shock on my face when I retrieved her. As I brought her back into the warmth of our home, it seemed to be a comfort that did not occur to her at all, just as the cold outside had not occurred to her during her flashy winter dance. Consider this analogy, a somewhat intoxicated mentality in a three-year-old body. Many more comedies occurred due to her size and physical abilities.

After her flashy winter dance, I feared that Sarah would attempt similar escapades and end up hurt or dead. Kids today, right? At the advice of some friends, we finally placed safety latches on the doors leading to the outside as a proactive measure. I guess I was so tired from reacting that I needed their advice to be proactive. Those latches caused Sarah to make a good amount of noise while she tried to get out, and the noise made us aware of her attempted escapes. Even with that present fear alleviated, a relentless and more ongoing fear remained my considerations of Sarah's future. Jeff and Jana's future did not obsessively preoccupy my thoughts, but since the experts already told me Sarah's future, I gave myself permission to worry; a lot. Rejecting the notion of one day at a time for Sarah caused me to fall into a depression. Admittedly, an occasional lowly mood hits every person, but for the next many years, my waking thought every morning would be that of Sarah not being able to get along in the world without needing protection. One day during this period, I attempted to settle for the day by watching one of those news programs, like *20/20* or *Prime Time*. The story reported about how individuals with disabilities, who are living in institutions, suffer victimization from people who work in them. I watched for a couple of minutes and then walked upstairs and went straight to bed. I cried until I fell asleep, and awoke the next morning with the thought that Sarah must remain with us. That very thought allowed comfort. Queen Sarah's diagnosis would affect how we all lived on a daily basis. Learning to live with that fact allowed for very big next steps in her growth, and the family's.

୧∾ର

Chapter 2: She Could Learn

From preschool to in-home program, 1995 through 1996 (three to four years old). Observing in Sarah's classroom gave me knowledge about what to utilize and practically apply in our home. The methods that gave her success proved that she could learn, and that was good! We consistently supported the same successful methods at home and preschool, and that comforted Sarah. Speech therapy made her frustrated at times, but patience allowed each small success to build upon another. We discovered Sarah had taught herself sign language by watching Barb interact with a hearing impaired child in the same classroom, and this confirmed the importance of visual aids in the teaching process.

> *(2/21/96) Classroom journal entry: The mystery of the signing is solved. But for Sarah to pick up signing from the little she has observed it used with Katie is really great! The other words Katie uses are "finished" and "help." Sarah sat at table to Play Peek-a-Boo Zoo, to do a puzzle and some form boards. She also did some playing with the small dollhouse. Nice appropriate play with the furniture and characters. (Barb)*

Incorporation of sign language encouraged speech from Sarah. If she signed "more", she said it. If she signed "all done", she said it. Visual cues helped Sarah to utter beginning sounds in words. Ability to utter the beginning sound resulted in her ability to say the whole word. That result caused me to consider my own nightmares, when I needed to get a phrase out, and had to force the first word out of my mouth with great effort, the complete phrase ensuing. An example of how the visual cues helped Sarah follows. I reminded her that the letter "m" goes "mmmm" while running an index finger across my lips and making the "mmmm" sound. She watched as I said, "mmmm, mom", and then she mimicked. That little help with the beginning sound gave her the push to say the whole word. There is a cue for each letter of the alphabet and those cues worked. One time I asked a speech therapist about the use of this technique and she said not to use it, and to instead push for whole words. I pushed for whole words for over a year and did not get them until I used this method! I guess one just never knows for sure. I just appreciate the fact that another speech therapist had tried the visual cues. We also encouraged speech by involving Sarah in activities that fed her need in the sensory department. Swinging, jumping, spinning, the teeter totter, or a good squeeze was all that she needed to encourage words like; more, stop, go, swing, spin, bounce, my turn, and your turn.

We hoped for signs of language development during her earliest years, and a couple of times Sarah uttered full sentences. One time Steve and I left Sarah with my grandma for a couple of minutes. When we got back, Granny Susan informed me that Sarah started crying and saying, "I want my Mommy." I did not believe it for a while, but I started to when a similar thing happened while my mom had Sarah for an entire weekend. Sarah said, "Get out of here!" while Grandma Patsy was following her to the kitchen. Perhaps Sarah was imitating how Grandma would scoot the pets out of the kitchen - Grandma felt it was not imitation. Yet another time, as I was settling Sarah for bed she said, "Jana" (and then made the noise for snoring). They shared a room at the time. I was so encouraged by that humor. Even before speech therapy, I noted that she did not engage in saying words, but she certainly liked singing them. I remember her singing Whitney Houston's Shoop, Shoop song and she seemed to know a lot of the words. I engaged in lyrical fill in the blank songs with Sarah; I would sing, "The wonderful thing about Sarah, is Sarah's a wonderful thing... But the most wonderful thing about Sarah is she's the only one. Yes, sheeeeee's_____" and then Sarah would sing "The only one". (Modified version of a song about Disney's Tigger.) I have read that we utilize differing areas of the brain as we talk or sing.

When Sarah first started preschool she did not even sit still for a minute. Those first days of preschool, the teachers directed her to complete tasks that they divvied up in baskets. To me, the baskets seemed to provide predictability, possibly because each basket represented the beginning, middle, and end of a task. Sarah seemed less anxious and less resistant toward the basket tasks and their completion. She learned to engage in required tasks, and to focus for longer durations of time; I associate that success to the basket tasks. Two minutes of focus became twenty minutes of focus as the school year progressed. Anything that was highly visual, or represented speech and language pathology helped her.

Since a mom had advocated for Applied Behavior Analysis (ABA) techniques for teaching her son, Barb received training in some of those methods right before Sarah's placement in preschool. She started a process of introducing Sarah to bits of ABA type teaching and those trials were successful. The trial teaching seemed to provide the kind of discernable instruction that Sarah needed, since it catered to her skills in imitation, love of predictability, and need for the manipulative and visual. It broke down skill acquisitions into portions from which Sarah could learn. Unfortunately, around this time there seemed to be some disagreements between TEACCH advocates and ABA advocates. When I made known the fact that I was considering ABA-type in-home teaching, some professionals who knew Sarah seemed uncomfortable. At the time, the district predominantly utilized TEACCH—it might have been that families had advocated for that method. In retrospect, the striking thing about the differing teaching techniques is that some were vigorously packaged and sold, many times at unrealistic costs for most families.

Sarah's positive response to the ABA-type techniques in the preschool room made a good argument for utilizing the program in our home. I contacted an out of state agency, and asked for information about the steps in beginning the process of ABA in-home programming. The agency required the recent administration of a battery of tests on Sarah, by whoever would do them. It determined candidacy by reviewing outcome of the assessments and test scores; and that seemed to indicate that she needed to be high functioning, or why bother. The school district performed all of the needed tests about a year before, but that was not recent enough for the agency. Since formal district assessment was only required every third year, some school district professionals were not available to do the required updated assessments; but other professionals in the district helped, for the good of Sarah. The assessments we lacked required appointments with specialists who were booked months in advance. When I finally had all the requirements fulfilled, I sent the results to the agency. After that, the agency called and told me they did not have anyone to send along to provide facilitation. I took Sarah to school after that call, and while I dropped her off, I vented at Barb. She knew about my excitement in awaiting the new help. I told her about the agency's waiting list. It was not there when I made the initial phone call to them, and I know this because I specifically asked about a waiting list, three times. I rambled on, "Blah, blah, vent, vent, and snort!", but then I became more constructive and began thinking aloud. "Why can't you run the program Barb? You have the training, and you run the ones in the school. Will you at least think about it?" With that, I came down from my frustration, because many suffered similar disappointment as agencies tried to accommodate a growing number of requests for help. For me, providence became evident, upon the enlightening consideration that Barb was the answer that had been staring me in the face all along. Said another way, perhaps the good Lord had a better idea.

Alongside the new and improved revelation was the fact that the clock kept ticking. Most experts proclaimed that therapy only truly worked when implemented on the very young. When I say worked, I mean it only normalized these children. When I say normalized, I guess that means cured. Sarah was already in her late threes! At the time, I still had my mind on normalization. Barb took time to consider. I think the biggest thing to consider was that the program lasted for two years. That was quite a commitment. Still, one day in March, as I dropped Sarah off at preschool, Barb consented to give it a try.

෴

Ann Dunham

Jana & Sarah

Chapter 3: Fancy Talk

In-home programming to kindergarten year, 1996 through 1999 (four to six years old). I actually wanted to have control over facilitation of our hour-intensive program. During this hopeful time, the district had an emerging ability to provide the personnel and consistency of hours professed as necessary for effective ABA type programming. The school provided an exceptional preschool class for Sarah, and that piece continued to be very important; but a whole district facilitating meaningful ABA for various students with differing degrees of delay remains an overwhelming proposition. During this time, the solidly built programs had university affiliations. Universities seemed to have an abundant personnel pool to draw from in the form of professors and students, and that probably facilitated a greater ability to provide intensity in teaching. While school districts need to come up with money for both facilitators and therapists, the universities already have the professors on staff and the therapists they use probably pay tuition in order to be involved in teaching autistic children. The hour-intense teaching goal seemed to be normalization of the affected children, to the point of integration in public school, at which time most if not all of the signs of their problems would no longer be evident. My understanding for that time was that the most touted ABA-type program would only accept higher-functioning autistics.

Even as our area did not have hour-intensive ABA type programming available, it did have many college students. Our personnel pool came from the local colleges in our area. I put up notices and it did not take long for the phone to start ringing. Barb interviewed every individual who called. Those to be included in our program had majors in speech and language, education, psychology, music, and physical training. We held a weekend workshop in our home. Not only did the ones we hired come to the workshop, other local professionals who expressed an interest attended as well. Barb gave a presentation of issues in autism and subsequently facilitated hands on training. After the workshop, she sat in on sessions with each therapist until she determined they had the competency and comfort required for the teaching process. Once our in-home program was in force, the team met every week to review data, determine progress, and maintain consistencies. When needed, implementation of next steps occurred.

Sarah's in-home program included the following: Discrete-trials, hour-intensive massed trials, naturalistic behavioral strategies, incidental teaching, preschool, and pivotal response. During the sessions, the therapist would present Sarah with discrete/massed trials (drills), but they also engaged her in a predetermined fun activity between drills. The fun activity involved the therapist utilizing a more naturalistic, incidental teaching strategy. Pivotal response was represented in the process, as elimination of some stimulatory behaviors appeared to coincide with Sarah's acquisition of new skills. My knowledge about the names of these strategies did not come about because I am educated in the field. I figured out the stuff we did had these names after reading a book about educating kids like my daughter. Before reading *Educating Children with Autism*, I would have told you that Sarah did drills, got play breaks, and seemed to stop doing so much stimulatory behavior while she was learning. Barb explained the ideas of ABA, discrete-trial training, behavioral modification, and whatever else one wants to call it.

(8/99) In-home report: The behavioral intervention home program that Sarah was involved in was one of behavior modification based on operant conditioning theory. This type of programming is also known as ABA (Applied Behavior Analysis) or discrete trial training. When behavior modification is used with children with autism, the child's behaviors are divided into deficits and excesses. Skills which are deficient are taught and behaviors that are excessive are decreased. Each skill to be taught is broken down into its most simple individual components. The child is then prompted to exhibit the desired simple skills and rewarded for success. Prompts may be

used initially to elicit the behavior then are gradually removed so that the child is able to demonstrate independent performance of the behavior. As a result, the behavior is strengthened and gradually acquired. Once individual components of the behavior have been acquired, each component is chained together to produce behaviors which are more complex and functional.

As new behaviors are learned, inappropriate behaviors are not rewarded. As a result, these inappropriate behaviors decrease in strength and gradually extinguish. This results in inappropriate behaviors being replaced by more functional and desirable behaviors which enable the child to more successfully communicate and learn.

I mention intensive ABA with regard to the in-home program, and it represented a rather large piece. The in-home program Barb set up was a combination of the Lovaas program found in *Teaching Developmentally Disabled Children, The ME Book* by Ivar Lovaas, the program described in *Let Me Hear Your Voice* by Catherine Maurice, and the behavioral program in *Behavioral Intervention for Young Children with Autism,* edited by Catherine Maurice. The program also had components derived from information gained by Barb through three ABA training workshops, two from CARD (Center for Autism and Related Disorders), and one from (WEAP) Wisconsin Early Autism Project. We had the benefit of these components coupled with Barb's many years of experience in the classroom with kids like Sarah! The fact that all of these strategies became a part of our hour-intensive program before a rather global recommendation by many experts in *Educating Children with Autism,* holds up Barb's competence as a facilitator. Some in our community and some out of state agencies found it necessary to question the integrity and meaningfulness of what we did. That was a drag. What was great was the fact that Sarah experienced happiness and she learned a lot. There was power behind what Barb had taught in the workshop. She lived what she taught and passed her knowledge on to others who were just beginning in their professional journey. For the years that followed, the therapists brought great joy to our family. It was a time of much positive focus, with the in-home teaching team bringing a great deal of growth and love into our littlest one's life. Jeff and Jana were included in the mix, as they sometimes worked alongside the therapists to help Sarah. Upon the first year anniversary of our in-home program, I shared some reflections with the therapists.

> I remember how hard it was for Sarah to talk at first, when therapy began. She has come so far. Even before the in-home program, Sarah had daily speech sessions. We tried sign language, visual cues, pictures and just about anything to get Sarah to use words. The fact that she is talking like she is, is nothing short of an answer to my prayers. There have been great gains. With every child being different there is no set way to teach them. In Sarah's case, the ABA type in home therapy seemed to be just the right thing for her. So far, it has worked but we have another year to go. This next year might be a bigger challenge since it gets into big time language (receptive, expressive and very social communicative exchanges).
> I really did not think we would get the in-home program to fly. I did not think we would find enough people to both commit, and then stay long term. I have considered all of you to be absolute angels for your time and patience with Sarah. You are all an answer to months of prayer. I have been blessed by your devotion to Sarah. I pray for great futures for all of you. Because of all that you have done for Sarah, she will have a chance at a better future. She loves all of you. I know because she has told me so.

The Preschool Language Scale (PLS) was administered to Sarah at a speech and language disorders clinic at about the same time as we celebrated our one year anniversary. The PLS is a test of communicative function. This was a happenstance thing, as we had not planned to have the comparison of scores. Chance as it was, Barb and I became happy with the results. We compared the language clinic's score to a two-year earlier administration of the same test by the school district, and the results showed much improvement.

TEST DATE: 11/5/96
Auditory Comprehension – Raw score: 9 (0 years, 10 months)
Expressive Communication – Raw Score: 17 (1 year, 8 months)

Ann Dunham

TOTAL LANGUAGE SCORE – 26 (1 year, 4 months)
Sarah was one month shy of four years old here.
TEST DATE: 4/7/98
Auditory Comprehension – Raw Score: 29 (2 years, 11 months)
Expressive Communication – Raw Score: 25 (2 years, 9 months)
TOTAL LANGUAGE SCORE – 54 (2 years, 9 months)
Sarah was five years and three months on this test date.
Higher scores and more even development were documented.

Success from the first year seemed to provide needed staying power for the therapists, in as much as they persevered through the second year. While the second year seemed to rush by for me, the therapists daily sat in the room doing the drills with Sarah. I am sure the second year did not fly by for them. Their dedication and perseverance are the biggest part of what facilitated growth for Sarah. Most of the therapist stayed throughout both years with her. After two years, I surveyed them to find out their impressions about her. I did not let them put their names on the surveys so the answers could be as candid as they wanted them to be.

Sarah During Therapy Years

Ann Dunham

1) Before working with Sarah, what knowledge did you have of her condition?
- ❖ None.
- ❖ None.
- ❖ I didn't know a whole lot. Just some basic characteristics, such as common signs and behavior they exhibit.
- ❖ Rainman, that is it. Well, also thought they were in their own little world. Lots of repetitive behavior and little speech. I had observed some kids.
- ❖ Was familiar because I worked with a boy who had the same condition.
- ❖ None.

2) How did you feel when working with Sarah?
- ❖ I was finding out a lot more about children then I ever knew before.
- ❖ Good. Sarah was much easier to communicate with than the other individual I worked with. Although she had no verbal, her actions were good describers (mime like).
- ❖ It would be a challenge. I didn't know if it was right for me.
- ❖ I heard about it from my professor. I was interested right away and wanted to start therapy but didn't have time. You wanted me to come and observe. I was not sure I would be able to handle it, but I was bound and determined from the very start. I knew there would be difficult and challenging times, but I prepared for that.
- ❖ Intimidated, and wondering how it was going to go.
- ❖ Really good experience. I thought it would be, as it was the area I was exploring as a possible career.

3) What was your first impression of Sarah, and if therapy would work?
- ❖ I thought she was really cute. I also thought if the therapy hadn't worked for other kids like Sarah that Steve, Ann and Barb wouldn't try it.
- ❖ What a cutie! I really had no thought on if the therapy would work.
- ❖ I remember Laura and Sarah talking about Sarah. About how she was. She was showing signs of improvement. I knew she was loved

*by all the therapists. I guess I knew that therapy would work since
I already heard progress reports from my friends. I remember
my first impression when I sat across the table from Sarah. I was
nervous…looking at Sarah and thinking that she has a lot to
teach me.*

- ❖ *I didn't think therapy would work. I wasn't sure if it would be
  successful. I was fascinated with Sarah. She seemed to have a high
  energy level, and seemed happy.*
- ❖ *Sarah appeared intelligent, and I thought in time Sarah would both
  improve in language and fine motor skills.*
- ❖ *She looked just like a normal girl. I didn't know if therapy would
  work or not.*

4) *What has been your most vivid triumph while working with Sarah?*
- ❖ *Seeing her play Old MacDonald with both hands (piano).*
- ❖ *Well, the way her language has sprouted has got to be one of the
  most amazing things I have seen. More personally, the first time
  she came up to me and wanted a "squeeze" (hug). I knew she had
  accepted me.*
- ❖ *When she started to know my name. Especially when she really
  started to interact and play with me, sometimes initiating play
  herself.*
- ❖ *One of the most vivid triumphs while working with Sarah was when
  we were going to do a drill Sarah didn't like…as I got it out she
  said, "No thank you." It made me realize that she understands a
  lot more than I had thought. It was so neat that she could express
  herself in that way, even though the answer was not what I was
  looking for.*

5) *What kept you going on a bad day?*
- ❖ *There has gotta be a better day…just kidding. It was a challenge.*
- ❖ *Knowing that she had the capability of doing better.*
- ❖ *I never took a bad session personally or let it get me down. I have
  seen so many positive things emerge from Sarah. I have always
  known that she is capable of doing much. I feel such a commitment
  to Sarah and want to help her all I can.*

- ❖ *It is because she is a friend, and I learn so much from Sarah. She is the most interesting person I know. I still question it sometimes, but I know persistence and consistency will help the program be successful.*
- ❖ *That with time things would improve and they always did.*
- ❖ *Sarah's all knowing smile, like she knew exactly what was going on.*

6) *Tell me about your worst session:*
- ❖ *Constant screaming, yelling and crying. She was so frustrated. I just wanted to hug her.*
- ❖ *Completed only two drills. Sarah was very unfocused, wouldn't talk and would kick her legs out and scream.*
- ❖ *She just cried…and it was stressful for me. Queasy stomach.*
- ❖ *One time I got so frustrated, I had swelled eyes, but it was mostly due to stress in my own life.*
- ❖ *Tantrums the first half and second half, spacey and wouldn't do anything.*
- ❖ *She was completely indifferent and nothing I did or said had an effect on her.*

7) *Would you consider the ABA, Behavior Modification, Discrete Trial (or whatever else you want to call it) played a major role in Sarah's improvement?*
- ❖ *I think therapy played a huge role in Sarah's improvement. I also think the hours spent teaching (no matter the type of teaching) played a big part.*
- ❖ *Yes. A huge major improvement.*
- ❖ *By all means. Yes. I believe that it has played a major role in shaping her life/behavior in the past year that I have worked with Sarah.*
- ❖ *For sure. Especially after I came back from summer break. I noticed a world of improvement. I was so excited to see how far therapy had taken Sarah.*
- ❖ *Yes.*
- ❖ *Yes, absolutely.*

8) Do you love Sarah?
- ❖ Very much. She is a wonderful funny girl. I have learned a lot from her.
- ❖ Sarah is one of those kids one never forgets.
- ❖ Yes. I really like her, and making sincere real contact with her.
- ❖ I love Sarah so much. I know that as a therapist I have taught her a lot, but she has taught me a lot too! I know I am going to miss her next year when I move off to who knows where.
- ❖ Yes. Very much so.
- ❖ Yes. I love Sarah. She is a sweet little girl and has taught me many things about patience and perseverance.

The individuality of the respondents lends quite a bit of authenticity to the survey, and I love how their personalities shone through in the responses. From the first year to the second, they reached some tall mountaintops with Sarah. The harder language drills tested the therapist as much as they tested Sarah, representing some valleys to the therapists. Typical use of language, expressive and receptive, proved to be an ongoing challenge Sarah. We felt it important to journal about Sarah's language successes all along the way. A review of some journal notes reflects the programming's influence, its technique becoming evident in her communication and comprehensive abilities.

> You came and took my egg salad sandwich from me, took a bite and spit it out. You handed the sandwich back and said, "Its okay. I'm alright." (5/4/98 Daddy)

> You lost your first tooth today! It happened at school and you were very upset. You made Barb attempt to put tape on your tooth so you could put it back in. You were putting tape on your lip and jaw when you saw Daddy. Daddy showed you Jana's two missing teeth and told you, "Same." And you said, "Same," and scuttled off, as it seemed to be enough to settle things. (5/19/98 Daddy)

> Hi Barb and Rochelle. Sarah was funny last night. During her second hour of therapy with Sally she was non compliant and giggling uncontrollably. I was in there for a little bit trying to help, but began to see I was more of a hindrance. I told Sally, "I'm out of here, so

you guys can get something accomplished." As I left the room Sarah said, "You are a coward." It was a riot! In Dave and the Giant Pickle, the giant pickle says to the Israelites, "You are all cowards," when no one will fight him. That is where she got it. (9/10/98 journal entry)

I came home late tonight. You were very excited as you heard me drive up and you started saying, "Daddy." When I came in you were jumping up and down. Momma asked, "How do you feel?" and you answered, "Happy!" (11/30/98 Daddy)

A review of the in-home programming drills' outcomes accentuates Sarah's strengths, but also gives witness to her frailties at that time. Her strengths helped her through her upcoming kindergarten year. We also facilitated preparation for kindergarten by allowing Sarah to spend time in a kindergarten room at her preschool location. Additionally, she spent an extra year in preschool.

First In-Home Therapy "Drills" Overview
This overview will provide Pg# of the trial in Behavioral Intervention for Young Children with Autism (Maurice et al.) and then outcome, with some brief statements. I sometimes make note of what she mastered and generalized. Some she mastered but did not generalize. Mastery indicates some knowledge, but possibly more rote in form and therefore more easily lost if not applied in appropriate context in real life. Rote knowledge is memorization, not in depth understanding. A generalized skill is one applied in real life in appropriate context. We varied the order of the trials (drills) presentation so that Sarah did not trick us with her ability to memorize. When necessary we utilized mass, distracter, and discriminator. The instruction she followed was usually referred to as a command or cue. Please be advised that one must purchase Behavioral Intervention for Young Children with Autism, in order to receive comprehensive instructions and explanations of each lesson.

Hello, Dr. Wells

Page 74, Makes Eye Contact: Mastered and generalized. After mastery, we sometimes utilized the eye contact cue for prompt purposes when we needed to have eye contact. The cue was "Look at me." We were not so concerned on sustained eye contact. We just needed enough of a look to know that Sarah was attending to the therapist. I always had a little concern that eye contact could be either hurtful or threatening to Sarah due to some reports by those with her condition.

Page 75, Imitates Gross Motor Movements: Easily mastered and generalized. The command was "Do this." The activities were: Tap table (palms), clap hands, wave, place arms up, stomp feet, tap legs, shake head (like nod), cover face with hands, and tap shoulders.

Page 76, Imitates Actions with Objects: Mastered and generalized. "Do this" was the command. The activities were: Hit drum, put on hat, wipe mouth, feed cabbage patch doll, hold phone to ear, brush hair, rock doll, put coin in bank.

Page 77, Imitates Fine Motor Movements: Mastered and generalized. "Do this" was the command. The activities were: Open and close fingers together, clasp hands together, tap index fingers together, tap thumb, wiggle fingers, rub hands together, thumbs up, point index finger to palm, thumbs together, victory sign (peace), extend index finger, both hands with victory sign.

Page 78, Imitates Oral Motor Movements: Mastered and generalized. "Do this" was the command. The activities were: Open mouth, stick out tongue, put lips together, tap teeth together, blow, smile, pucker, place tongue on top teeth, place top teeth over lower lip.

Page 79, Follows One-step Instructions: Mastered and generalized. The activity was the cue. The activities were: Sit down, stand up, wave bye-bye, give me a hug, put arms up, clap your hands, turn around, jump, throw this away, blow a kiss, turn on the

light, shut the door, turn on the music, get a tissue, give me five, stomp your feet. (The order of the presentation of these varied.)

Page 80, Body Parts (Receptive and Expressive): *Mastered and generalized. The cue was "Touch_____." The activities were: Touch...nose, eyes, mouth, ear, hair, head, feet, cheeks, shoulders, hand, face, arm, fingers, toes, thumb, chin, tummy, and elbow.*

Page 82, Objects (Receptive and Expressive): *This was mastered and generalized. "Point to _____" and "What is this?" were the cues. The activities involved: Keys, shovel, doll, TV, trike, banana, balloon, juice, spaghetti, blocks, eggs, wagon, bath tub, cookies, pool, saw, hammer, pail, rocks, lamp, shampoo, vacuum, calendar, swim suit, crayon, movie, camera, paper, shirt, lego, peanut butter, play dough, magna doodle, napkin, knife, clock, shorts, bowl, book, cup, diaper, spoon, soap, dog, sock, toothbrush, car, hanger, pillow, towel, brush, shoe, coat, chair, table, blanket, airplane, pencil, bread, phone, swing, jammies. (We used the actual objects instead of pictures in this drill.)*

Page 83, Identifies Familiar People: *Mastered and generalized. The commands were "Point to _____" and "Go to _____." The activities involved: All family members, all schoolmates, and all school staff who worked with Sarah.*

Page 84, Verbs (Instructions and Picture Identification): *Mastered and generalized. The commands were "Show me_____," "Point to _____," and "What is the boy (or girl) doing?" The activities were: Sitting, standing, clapping, waving, eating, drinking, turning, hugging doll, kissing doll, jumping, blowing, sleeping, knocking, reading, drawing, brushing, throwing, walking, kicking, falling, climbing, riding, hopping, building, running, catching, laughing, dancing, crawling, picking up, pointing, talking, sweeping, playing, crying, lying down, listening, carrying, hiding, pulling, pushing, skipping, chasing, counting, looking, smiling. (Identification in pictures and real life.)*

Hello, Dr. Wells

Page 85, Environmental Objects (Receptive and Expressive): *Mastered and generalized. The commands were "Touch the _____" and "What is this?" The activities included: Table, chair, window, bed, carpet, curtain, light switch, floor, door, fridge, sink, stove, toilet, shower, stairs, desk, TV, couch, wall, fan (point to).*

Page 86, Points to Pictures in a Book: *Mastered and generalized. The commands were "Point to_____" and "What is this?" The activities included: Bugs Bunny, shoes, door, window, diaper, ball, tea, table, cow, horse, pig, chicken, sheep, sock, star, brush, dog, frog, goat, cat, rooster, owl, book, elephant, bear, rabbit, dear, hen, duck, milk, apple, watermelon, bread, tiger, kangaroo, orange, pillow, blanket, flower, Grover's hat, Grover's shirt, camel, boat, tree, shovel, heart, pig, Barney's hat, ABCD…, hat, swimming pool, swim suit, duck, Big Bird, banana, toothbrush, desk, paper, pencil, shapes, numbers, colors, head, scissors, blocks, cookies, drink, slide, swing, trike, brush, bath tub, spaghetti, penguin, hammer, lion, bed, airplane.*

Page 87, Function of Objects (Receptive and Expressive): *Mastered and generalized. The cues were "What do you _____?" The activities included: Write with, drink from, eat with, cut with, read with, sleep in, sit on, talk on, color with, wash with, point with, blow nose with, sweep with. (And then "What do you do with _____?" soap, tissue, a phone, a broom.)*

Page 88, Possession (Receptive and Expressive): *Mastered and generalized. The cues were "Touch _____" and then "Whose _____?" The activities included: Momma's shoes, Sarah's arm, Momma's shirt, Sarah's nose, Momma's hair, Momma's arm, Sarah's feet, Gina's pants, Jana's shirt, Jana's shoes, Sarah's pants, Steve's hand, Steve's thumb, Steve's shirt, April's pants, April's shirt, Sarah's foot, Jeff's shirt, Jeff's hair, Jeff's shoe, Jeff's sock, Jana's hair, Bugs Bunny's eye, Ernie's eye (ear, mouth, shirt, shoes, pants), girl's eye (ear, hair), Sarah's head, Sarah's toes (etc.), Sarah's tummy, Jana's nose (cheeks, elbow, hair, feet, tummy), Barney's toes (etc.), Bugs Bunny's ears (feet, arms, nose, diaper).*

Ann Dunham

Page 93, Labels Familiar People: Mastered and generalized. The cues were "Point to _____" and "Touch _____," then "Who is this?" and "Give me _____." The activities involved the following people: Jana, Jeff, Daddy, Uncle Wayne, David, Barb, Rochelle, Cheryl, April, Gina, Jessica, Zarina, Leah, Steve, Sally, Britt, Laura, classmates. (Present picture of person, then present written name of person, match them correctly and then read the name.)

Page 95, Social Questions: Mastered. The actual question is the cue. The following were presented: What is your name?, How old are you?, How are you today?, Where do you live?, Who is your sister?, Who is your brother?, What do you like to play with?, What is your daddy's name?, What do you like to eat?, What do you like to drink?, When is your birthday?, What's your mom's name?, What's your favorite movie?, Where do you go to school?, What's your teacher's name?, Who's your friend?, Who's your daddy?, Who's your mommy?, Who's your teacher?, What is your address?, What is your phone number?

Page 96, Verbs (Labels in Pictures, Others, Self): Mastered and generalized. The cue was the question "What am I doing?" The activities involved: Standing, sitting, clapping, waving, eating, drinking, turning, jumping, hugging, kissing, blowing, sleeping, knocking, reading, drawing.

Page 97: Matches: Mastered and generalized. Matching was definite 100 percent strength for Sarah. The command was "Match."

Page 98, Colors (Receptive and Expressive): Mastered and generalized. The cues were "Point to _____" and "What is this?" The activities included: Blue, black, red, yellow, green, white, purple, orange, pink, and brown. (Shapes and objects were added as a form of distracter. When presented with the question "What color is it?" we needed Sarah to give us the color and not identify the shape or object.)

Modified Version of 98, Read Color Words: *Mastered and generalized. It was done like this: The question "What color?" and then the cue "Find same" followed with the therapist showing word cards with the color name written in the color's actual color. The response by Sarah was to find the color match or crayon match. Then the therapist would hold up the card with the printed color name and cue with "Read." Upon mastery of the preceding steps, the therapists would show the color word written in the color's actual color and have Sarah find the color word written in black (red written in black for instance) that matched. "Find same" was the cue for that.*

Page 99, Shapes (Receptive and Expressive): *Mastered and generalized. The cues were "Point to_____" and "What is this?" The activities involved: Circle, square, triangle, rectangle, diamond, oval, star, heart.*

Page 100, Letters (Receptive and Expressive): *Mastered and generalized. The commands were "Touch _____," "Point to_____," and "What letter is it?" The activities included all letters.*

Modified Version of 100, Phonetic Sounds and "Write": *Mastered and generalized. Sarah made each letter's phonetic sound—long and short for the vowels. Additionally Sarah learned to write each letter via "Do this" cue while the therapist wrote the letter and then used the command "Write," at which time Sarah would write the letter. The activity involved all letters.*

Page 101, Numbers (Receptive and Expressive): *Mastered and generalized. The commands were "Point to _____" and "What number is it?" This activity involved all numbers.*

Modified Version of 101: *Mastered and generalized. Sarah counted objects or tallies via the command "Count." Additionally, Sarah learned to rote count up to one hundred. Sarah learned to write all the numbers via "Do this," and then "Write," the same as the letters.*

Page 102, Imitating Gross Motor Movements While Standing*: Mastered and generalized. The command was "Do this." The activities were: Jump up and down, turn around, put arms out, march, sit on floor, bang hands on floor, knock door, walk around chair, lay on floor, put hands on hips, twist at the waist, touch toes, run and stop, lift one foot up, hop, fly like an airplane, crawl under the table, lift up the chair, kick a ball.*

Page 103, Imitates Sequence (Gross Motor Actions with Objects)*: Mastered and generalized. The command was "Do this." The activities:*
- ✓ *Clap hands, then hit table*
- ✓ *Hands to hips, then hands to head*
- ✓ *Knock two times, then wave*
- ✓ *Whee on slide, then hammer two times*
- ✓ *Ring bell, then hit hammer*
- ✓ *Slap knees, then clap hands*

Page 104, Imitates Actions Paired with Sounds*: Mastered and generalized. The therapist used the cue "Do this" while modeling the following actions:*
- ✓ *Put toy down slide while saying, "Whee."*
- ✓ *Hammer while saying, "Bang bang."*
- ✓ *Telephone and say, "Hello."*
- ✓ *Push car and say, "Zoom."*
- ✓ *Play with lion and say, "Roar."*
- ✓ *Play with piano while saying, "Lalalala."*
- ✓ *Hold frog and say, "Ribbit."*
- ✓ *Hold snake and say, "Ssssss."*

Page 105, Imitates Block Patterns*: Mastered and generalized. The therapist cued with, "Build this," and would build structures with blocks and then Sarah would replicate them.*

Page 106, Copies Simple Drawings*: Mastered and generalized. The therapist drew something and then said, "Draw_____." The therapist drew the following: Vertical line, horizontal line, plus sign, circle,* *diagonal line, straight line letters, numbers, shapes, smiley face, flower, car, house, person, rainbow, and people Sarah knew. This drill prepared Sarah for writing letters and numbers via the "Do this," "Write____," or "Draw____" command.*

Page 107, Rooms (Expressive and Receptive): *Mastered and generalized. The therapist cued with, "Go to____," and then went to that room with Sarah. The following rooms were part of the activity: Kitchen, bedroom, Sarah's room, bathroom, Jeffrey's room, Jana's room, downstairs, living room, back yard. The therapist would also have pictures of each room and cue with, "What's this?" and Sarah would respond with the name of the room in the picture. The room name was also written on cards so that Sarah could either match pictures of the room with the name for that room, or simply retrieve the written room name and hand it to the therapist at her request.*

Page 108, Emotions (Receptive): *Mastered and generalized. The therapist had pictures of people showing different emotions. The cue was "Point to____" or "Show me____" and Sarah would either point to the proper picture with that emotion on it, or she would demonstrate the emotion herself ("Show me"). The following emotions were represented: Happy, sad, angry, silly, mad, scared, and surprised.*

Page 109, Places (Receptive and Expressive): *Mastered and generalized. The therapist used the cues "Point to____" and "What is this a picture of?" Sarah either responded by pointing to the picture of the place, or giving the verbal response if asked what it was a picture of. The following places were represented: Park, Burger King, Dairy Queen, School, classroom, Disney Store, zoo.*

Page 110, Follows Two-Step Instructions: *Mastered and generalized. The cue was "Go to the____and get____." The activities involved the following: Bathroom/soap, bathroom/brush, bathroom/towel, bathroom/cup, bathroom/toothbrush, kitchen/spoon,* kitchen/cup, kitchen/bowl, bathroom/shampoo, kitchen/fork, kitchen/ napkin, kitchen/dishtowel, bathroom/Band-Aid.

Page 111, Gives Two Objects (and three): Mastered and generalized. The cues were "Give me the _____ and the _____," and then "Give me the _____, _____ and _____." The following objects were available to pull from in a basket: Book, shoe, cup, peanut butter, camera, diaper, movie, brush, sock, dog, towel, swimsuit, car, tape, ball, hanger, shirt, and phone.

Page 112, Attributes (Receptive and Expressive): Mastered and generalized. The cues were "Touch_____," "Point to_____," and "What is this?" The activities involved the following attributes: Wet, dry, wet diaper, wet washcloth, dry diaper, dry washcloth, dry paper, hot, cold, hot cup, cold cup, big, little, clean, dirty, big shoes, little shoes, big ball, little ball, clean cup, dirty cup, clean sock, dirty sock, empty, full, cup of legos (full), empty cup, soft, hard, soft pillow, hard wood, hard rock, hard brick, soft cotton, soft stuffed animal, long, short, long string, short string, long spoon, short spoon, long pencil, short pencil, long paper, short paper, opened, closed, opened window, closed window, opened door, closed door, opened drawer, closed drawer, opened Pooh tree house, closed Pooh tree house, opened headboard cupboard, closed headboard cupboard, opened closet, closed closet, smooth, rough, smooth table, smooth book, smooth box, smooth rock, rough shell, sough sandpaper.

Page 113, Community Helpers (Receptive and Expressive): Mastered and generalized. The cues were "Point to_____," and "Who is this?" with mass and discriminator. The therapist would place pictures of community helpers on the table and tell Sarah to go through them. Then the therapist would pick one to show to Sarah and cue with, "Who is this?" or ask Sarah to "Point to" a particular community helper. This activity included: Firefighter, police officer, mail carrier, teacher, farmer, doctor, waiter, and dentist. Sometimes Sarah would say, "Policeofficesarah," for police officer!

Hello, Dr. Wells

Page 114, Pretends: Mastered and generalized. The cue was "Pretend you are_____." The activities were: Drinking, brushing hair, washing face, brushing teeth, licking ice cream cone, driving a car, sweeping, putting on a hat, a snake, a lion, a crow, a dog, a monkey, a rabbit, a frog, a cat, a bird, a bee, an airplane.

Page 115, Categories (Matches, Identifies, and Labels): Mastered and generalized. The cues were "Touch_____," "What is this?" and "_____ is a _____." The therapist cued with, "Touch_____," and then Sarah touched the plate at which point the therapist cued with, "What is this?" and Sarah responded, "Plate is a dish." The activity included: Food, clothes, animals, toys, fruit, tools, vegetables, transportation, instruments, furniture, shapes, colors, appliances, dishes.

Page 116, Pronouns (My and Your): Mastered. The cue was "Touch (my or your) _____." The activity included: Ears, eyes, feet, hair, mouth, nose, tummy, cheeks, fingers, and shirt.

Page 117, Prepositions (Receptive and Expressive): Mastered. The cues were "Put (color block) _____ on (color block) _____" and after doing so, the cue was "Where is the _____?" with the answer being one of the prepositions. The following prepositions were involved: Between, under, next to, in front of, in back of, in, on, behind, over. We did this with people as well.

Page 118, Identifies/Labels Objects When Described (In and Out of View): Mastered and generalized. The cue was "I am thinking of something that is_____" and then "What is it?" The activity included: Apple (red, grows on a tree, you can eat it, it is a food), ball (round, it bounces, you can throw it, it is a toy), carrot (long, it is orange, you can eat it, it is a vegetable), banana, shoe, cat, frog, car, phone, spoon, cow, bird, fork, pajamas, bed, napkin, crayon, cup, shoe, peanut butter, towel, pillow, jet, wagon, trike.

Page 119, Sequence Cards (Puts in Order and Describes): Mastered and generalized. The cue was "Put in order" and then "Tell me a story." The activity included: Pumpkin Story, Seed Story,

Ann Dunham

Brushing Teeth Story, Writing a Letter Story, The Slide Story, Winter Story, Getting Ready for School Story, The Boy is Riding a Bike Story, Mom is Going to the Store Story, How to Make an Apple Tree Story, Harvesting Corn Story, Going on a Picnic Story, How to Make an Easter Egg Story.

Page 120, Gender (Receptive and Expressive): *Mastered and generalized. The cues were "Point to _____ "and "What is this?" Easily mastered using a variety of presentations to do with boys and girls.*

Page 121, Answers Wh-questions about Objects and Pictures: *Mastered and generalized. The cues were "What is this?", "What color is it?", "What do you do with it?", and "What is a_____?"The activity included: Banana, apple, shoe, ball, book, coat, towel, peanut butter, potato, sock, mitten, cup, shirt, pillow, iron, toaster, bubbles, soap, Kleenex, doll, shampoo, brush, spoon, cereal, plate, fork, hat, blanket, pencil, toothbrush, puzzle.*

Page 121, *Done with pictures: Mastered and generalized. The cues were "What is happening (in the pictures)?"The following were target statements that we looked for from Sarah: The boy and the girl are playing in the mud, The children are playing with the guinea pigs, The boys are playing on the slide, The children are fighting over the cereal, The mom is pushing the boy on the swing, The girl pushed the blocks over, The children are planting a flower, The boy and his dad are planting seeds, The boy's dad pushed him down the sled in the snow, The children are playing London Bridges Falling Down, The girl is looking at the leaves, The boy is running very fast, The girl is playing in the water, The girl is talking to the puppet, The boy and girl are playing with the beads, The boy is talking on the telephone to his friend, The girl is silly. She put her sunglasses on upside down, The boy is playing on the floor with blocks, The kids are riding tricycles, The girl is hanging upside down, The children are clapping their hands, The boy is eating an apple, The girl is jumping rope, The boy is knocking on the door, The girl is painting a picture, The boy is sharing an animal cracker with his friend, The boy is pulling the girl's hair, The girls are watering the flower.*

Hello, Dr. Wells

Page 122, Yes/No (Objects): *Mastered and generalized. The cue was "Is this a ____?" with response being either "Yes" or "No." The activity included: Diaper, frog, camera, book, shoe, towel, peanut butter, hanger, apple, cup, Bugs Bunny, paper, pencil, and ball.*

Page 123, Function of Body Parts: *Mastered and generalized. The cues were "What do you____with?" and "What do you do with your ____?" The activity included: See/eyes, smell/nose, hear/ears, touch/hands, walk/legs, sneeze/nose, blink/eye, talk, mouth, kiss/lips.*

Page 124, Labels Emotions: *Mastered and generalized. The therapist asked, "How do I feel?" while facially displaying an emotion. This activity involved the following emotions: Angry, happy, sad, surprised, scared, sleepy, sick. Sarah loved this drill.*

Page 125, Categories (Labels Category & Names Objects in a Category): *Mastered and generalized. The therapist said, "Sort," "Point to food," "Point to animal," "What is this?" and "What is ____?" Example: "A____is a _____" (A parrot is a bird). The activity involved category cards with a variety of: food, animals, clothes, toys, shapes, colors, numbers, and letters.*

Page 126, Using Simple Sentences: *Mastered and generalized. Cue was "What is this?" with target statement from Sarah of "This is a ____." Next cue was "What do you see?" with target statement of "I see a ____." And cue of "What do you have?" with target statement of "I have a____." The activity included: Ball, peanut butter, shoe, diaper, sock, apple, frog, towel, book, blanket, camera, bottle, jammies, Barbie, cup, window, box, spoon, game.*

Page 127, Reciprocates Information (I Have...I See...): *This was mastered and generalized. The drill went as follows:*
T "I have a pig."
S "I have a frog."

T "My pig is pink."
S "My frog is green."

42

T "My pig can walk."
S "My frog can jump."

T "My pig is an animal."
S "My frog is an animal."

The activity included the following: Chicken/cow, ball/book, brush/comb, sock/hat, doll/Pumba, duck/cow, cup/spoon, and jet/boat.

Page 128, Reciprocates Social Information: Mastered and generalized. Activities included the following statements from Sarah: My name is Sarah, I am six years old, I live in Sioux Falls, I like to play with Bugs Bunny, My brother's name is Jeff, My sister's name is Jana, I like to eat popcorn, My friend's name is Eric, My mom's name is Ann, My dad's name is Steve, My favorite computer game is Dr. Seuss.

For reciprocal, it went as follows:
T "My name is _____."
S "My name is Sarah."

T "My birthday is____."
S "My birthday is Dec tenth."

T "I am ____ years old."
S "I am six years old."

T "My daddy's name is ____."
S "My daddy's name is Steve."

T "My mom's name is ____."
S "My mom's name is Ann."

T "My brother's name is _____."
S "My brother's name is Jeff."

T "My sister's name is _____."
S "My sister's name is Jana."

Hello, Dr. Wells

T "I live in _____."
S "I live in Sioux Falls."

T "My favorite food is _____."
S "My favorite food is french fries."

T "I like to _____ at the park."
S "I like to slide at the park."

T "My favorite video is _____."
S "My favorite video is Pink Panther."

T "My favorite restaurant is _____."
S "My favorite restaurant is Puerto Vallarta."

T "My favorite computer program is _____."
S "My favorite computer program is Grandma and Me."

Page 129, I Don't Know (Unknown Objects and Questions): *Mastered. The cue was "What is this?" with the target response from Sarah of "I don't know." We used familiar and unfamiliar objects. The target response was prompted at first until Sarah understood the expectation (as it is with all the trials). Eventually Sarah was able to express if she knew what something was via the response of "I don't know." She learned to respond with an answer of what the item was if she knew what it was.*

Page 130, Asks "What's that?": *Mastered. The cue was "Tell me what you see" and "What's that?" The activity included: Banana, apple, shoe, ball, book, coat, towel, peanut butter, potato, sock, mitten, cup, shirt, pillow, iron, toaster, bubbles, soap, Kleenex, doll, shampoo, brush, spoon, cereal.*

Page 134, Pronouns (He and She): *Mastered and generalized. Cue was "What is the (boy/girl) doing?" Pictures cards were used. Target response from Sarah was "(He/She) is jumping."*

44

Page 136, Describes Pictures in Full Sentences: Mastered. The cue was "Tell me about the picture" as Sarah was shown a picture. That would result in an approximation of target sentences that had been taught to her.

Page 138, Recalls Events (Immediate and Past with Delay): This was hard for Sarah. Cues were "Where did you go?" "What did you do?" and "Who did you see?" Sometimes she was able to do this, but it was not a strength.

Page 139, Answers "Where?" Questions: Mastered. The cue was "Where do you_____?" Involved: __go to sleep?, __take a bath?, __cook dinner?, __live?, __buy groceries?, __find a stove?, __play on a slide and swings?, __go to school?, __see a lion?, __go swimming?

Page 140, Function of Rooms: Cues were "What room do you_____in?" and "What do you do in the_____?" This involved: Kitchen/cook, bedroom/sleep, bathroom/bath, dining room/eat, downstairs/watch TV, basement/play Nintendo.

Page 141, Answers "When?" Questions: The cue was "When do you _____?" Involved: __go to sleep?, __take a bath?, __eat lunch?, __go to school?, __wake up?, __does it get dark?, __does the sun come up?, __go to the doctor?, __is your birthday?, __go swimming?, __go to church?, __see the sun?, __see the moon and stars?, __eat breakfast?, __drink?

Page 142, Delivers A Message: The therapist cued Sarah with "Go tell_____." It involved Sarah going and telling the following:

✓ Mom, I want a hug
✓ Mom, I want a kiss
✓ Dad, I want a drink
✓ Jana, I want a book.

Sarah loved this drill.

Hello, Dr. Wells

Page 143, Role Plays with Puppets: *Mastered and generalized. Sarah loved this drill. Interactions were:*

T "I am an elephant."
S "I am a lion."

T "My name is Ellie Elephant. What is your name?"
S "My name is Leo Lion."

T "How are you?"
S "I am fine."

T "I live in Africa. Where do you live?"
S "I live in Africa."

T "I am gray. What color are you?"
S "I am tan."

T "I have a short tail. Is your tail long or short?"
S "My tail is long."

T "I have great big ears. Are your ears big or little?"
S "My ears are little."

T "The sound I make is a trumpet. What sound do you make?"
S "I roar."

T "When I am hungry I eat plants. What do you eat?"
S "I eat meat."

T "It is time to go. Goodbye."
S "Good bye."

Page 144, Same and Different (Receptive): *Mastered. The cues were "Which ones are the same?" and "Which ones are different?" Random presentations of a vast variety of items.*

Page 145, Identifies What Does Not Belong (Attribute and Category): *Mastered. The cues were "Which one does not belong?" and "Which one is different?"*

Page 147, Answers Wh-Questions About Topics: *The therapist would ask a question and then Sarah would answer in the following way, or with some approximation that was close enough:*
T "What did you eat for breakfast?"
S "Pancakes."

T "When do you eat breakfast?"
S "In the morning."

T "Why do you eat breakfast?"
S "Because I am hungry."

T "Where do you eat breakfast?"
S "In the kitchen."

T "Who makes you breakfast?"
S "Mommy does."

T "When do you take a bath?"
S "At night."

T "Who gives you a bath?"
S "Daddy does."

T "Why do you have to take a bath?"
S "To get clean."

T "Where do you take a bath?"
S "In the bathtub."

T "Where do you go to school?"
S

Hello, Dr. Wells

T "Who do you see at school?"
S "Eric, Ricki, Nathan, Maggie, Timothy, Jimmy."

T "When do you go to school?"
S "Monday, Tuesday, Wednesday, Thursday."

T "What do you do when you are hungry?"
S "I eat food."

T "What do you do when you are sleepy?"
S "I go to bed."

T "What do you do when you are dirty?"
S "I take a bath."

T "What do you do when you are thirsty?"
S "I get a drink."

T "What do you do when you see something silly?"
S "I laugh."

T "What do you do when you are cold?"
S "I put on a sweatshirt."

T "What do you do when you fall down and hurt yourself?"
S "I tell Mom to put a band aid on."

T "When do you go to sleep?"
S "At night."

T "When do you take a bath?"
S "When I am dirty."

T "When do you eat dinner?"
S "At night."

T "When do you go to school?"
S "In the afternoon."

T "When do wake up?"
S "In the morning."

T "When does it get dark?"
S "It gets dark at night."

T "When does the sun come up?"
S "In the morning."

T "When is your birthday?"
S "Dec tenth."

Page 149, Finds Hidden Object Given Location Clues: *Mastered. The therapist would hide an object and then give clues about where it was. It started with one clue, but then built up to using four clues to find a variety of objects...even used prepositions as part of the process. Example: One clue (In the closet), two clues (in the closet, in a brown box), three clues (in the kitchen, under the table, in the red cup).*

Page 150, Discriminates When to Ask / When to Reciprocate: *Mastered. We had a couple sessions that had this sort of conversation line:*
T "Sarah."
S "What?"

T "I went somewhere last night."
S "Where did you go?"

T "I went to the movies. My favorite movie is _____."
S "My favorite movie is Veggie Tales."

T "I ate something at the movies.
S "What did you eat?"

T "I ate popcorn. I love popcorn."
S "I love it too."

Hello, Dr. Wells

T *"I love it with butter."*
S *"I love it with salt."*

T *"I saw someone at the movies."*
S *"Who did you see?"*

T *"I saw Mary. Mary is my best friend."*
S *"Ricki is my best friend."*

Page 151, Retells story: *Mastered. The therapist presented many stories like this one... One day Caitlin wrote a letter. Then she walked to the mailbox and put the letter in the mailbox. After presenting the story the therapist and Sarah would have an exchange:*
T *"Who wrote the letter?"*
S *"Caitlin."*

T *"Where did Caitlin go?"*
S *"To the mailbox."*

T *"What did Caitlin do?"*
S *"Wrote a letter."*

Page 152, Describes Topics: *Mastered. The cues were "Tell me about_____" and then Sarah provided appropriate responses. The following were represented:*
T *"School."*
S *"I go to School. My teacher's name is Barbara. I play with Ricki, Eric, Timothy, and Nathan."*

T *"Jeffrey."*
S *"My brother's name is Jeffrey. He is nine years old. He likes to skateboard."*

T *"Disney Store"*
S *"I go to the Disney Store with Mom. I watch the movie on the big screen. We look at all the toys. Mom buys one toy for me."*

T "Christmas."
S "It is a holiday. It comes in December. Santa comes and brings presents. I play in the snow."

Page 153, Tells a Story: *Mastered. The therapist would as Sarah to "Tell me about_____": Ball, shoe, rabbit, book, dog, and car. This was an attempt at having Sarah define words with simple descriptive sentences. The therapist would also have Sarah "Tell me about the book" with the following being represented: Cinderella, Car's Birthday, Snow White, Green Eggs and Ham, Dumbo. Questions were presented during "Tell me about the book" with the following being represented: What will _____ do?, How does He/ She feel?, What will happen?, Why is he/she (sad, angry, crying, happy)? The therapist would ask Sarah to, "Tell me a story," at which point Sarah would give approximations of mostly real life events that we turned into stories with the following being represented: Zarina Went to the Farm, Barbie Went to the Farm, Katie went to the Farm, Christmas Tree Story, Playing in the Snow, Going to McDonald's and Thanksgiving Story.*

Page 155, Expresses Confusion and Asks for Clarification: *This was mastered. The therapist would actually have to come up with things that Sarah had no knowledge of and then present a cue/question to Sarah. They would then have to prompt Sarah to say, "I don't understand. Please show me how to do that." Then the therapist would have to show Sarah how. In this drill the therapist had to present different cues/questions quite frequently in order to find things that Sarah would not understand since she would learn the proper response after her response of, "I don't understand. Please show me how to do that."*

Page 158, Uses Correct Tense: *Mastered. Cues were "What are you doing?" with Sarah's present tense responses (I am standing), "What did you do?" with a past tense response (I clapped), and "What are you going to do?" with a future tense response (I am going to eat).*

Hello, Dr. Wells

Page 160, Describes How: Mastered. Cue was "How do you_____?" and it involved: __brush your teeth?, __make a peanut butter and jelly sandwich?, __take a shower?, __dye an Easter Egg?, __fly a kite?, __go tubing?, __go swimming?. We actually started out by having Sarah do these activities so that Sarah could apply meaning to the situations.

Page 161, Same and Different (Expressive, In View): Mastered. The cues were "Why are these the same?" and "Why are these different?" A variety of objects were randomly presented in the context of "same" or "different."

Page 163, Answers "Which…?" Questions: Mastered. The cue was "Which_____" with the following being represented: One can swim?, toy can you throw?, food tastes sweet?, animal says roar?, season does it snow?, one do you wear on your head?, do you ride?, animal is soft and furry?, one is little?, one flies in the sky?

Page 165, Answers "Why…?" and "If…?" Questions: Mastered. The cues were "Why do you_____?" and "What do you do if you are _____?" with the following being represented: eat/hungry, drink/thirsty, sleep/tired, cry/sad, smile/happy, go to the doctor/sick, take a bath/dirty, put on a coat/cold, laugh/something is funny, use an umbrella/it is raining.

Page 166, Completes Sentences Logically: Mastered. The following are samples but not a complete list.
- ✓ He is hungry. He needs to _____(eat)
- ✓ It's raining. She needs an _____(umbrella)
- ✓ He is thirsty. He needs a _____(drink)
- ✓ The door is locked. She needs a ___(key)
- ✓ His hands are dirty. He needs to _____(wash them)
- ✓ She is tired. She needs to _____(go to sleep)
- ✓ She is sad. She is going to ___(cry)
- ✓ She is being tickled. She is _____(laughing)
- ✓ The paper is torn. He needs some_____(tape)
- ✓ She wants to draw. She needs _____(paper, pencil, chalk or crayons)

Ann Dunham

- ✓ She is happy. She is____(smiling)
- ✓ Sarah wants to swim. She needs to put on her ____(swim suit)
- ✓ It is snowing. She needs to put on her ____(coat)

Page 170, Excludes an Item Based on Attribute and Category: Mastered. Cue was "Give me something that's not ____." with the following represented: Colors, shapes, attributes (soft, hard, long, short), animal, food, clothing, letters, numbers.

BBSI: Begged, Borrowed and Stolen: The next drills represented either came from CARD or Barb just put them together because she knew the expectations at school.

A, Word Association: Mastered. Cues were "What goes with?" and "Why do____and ____go together?" The following are represented:
T "What goes with monkey?"
S "Banana."

T "Why do a monkey and banana go together?"
S "Because a monkey eats a banana."

T "What goes with a sock?"
S "A foot."

T "Why does a sock and foot go together?"
S "Because I put a sock on my foot."

B, Defines Objects: The cues were "Tell me what an apple is" and "Tell me about ____" with the following being represented: Apple, car, cat, popcorn, tree, bed, water.

C, Emotions: Went as follows: T "When you are ____(happy)" / S "I ____(smile)." The following are represented: Sad/I cry, silly/I giggle, scared/I run and hide, mad/I scream, frustrated/I get mad.

D, First / Last: Cues were "Point to first letter" and "Point to last letter."

Hello, Dr. Wells

E, First and Last Name: *Cues were "What is your first name?" and "What is your last name?" Sarah would either write the answer or say it.*

F, High Frequency Words: *Mastered. Sarah read the following words: a, about, after, all, an, and, are, as, at, be, been, but, by, called, can, could, did, do, down, each, find, first, for, from, had, has, have, he, her, him, his, how, I, if, in, into, is, it, its, just, know, like, little, long, made, make, many, may, more, most, my, no, not, now, of, on, one, only, or, other, out, over, people, said, see, she, so, some, than, that, the, their, them, then, there, these, they, this, time, to, two, up, use, very, was, water, way, we, were, when, where, which, who, will, with, words, would, you, your.*

H, Calendar: *Mastered. The therapist had Sarah read all words for the days of the weeks and the months. The therapist used the "Sort" command in order to have Sarah categorize the days and the months. Sarah put the days and months in proper sequence. The following happened during this drill:*
T "What day is it today?"
S "Today is _____."

T "What day was it yesterday?"
S "Yesterday was_____."

T "What will tomorrow be?"
S "Tomorrow will be_____."

T "Saturday is a _____."
S "Day."

T "January is a_____."
S "Month."

I, Numbers: *Mastered. A cue of "Count to____" would result in Sarah rote counting (up to 100). A cue of "How Many?" would result in Sarah counting tallies or objects and giving the answer.*

A cue of "What number?" would have Sarah reading the number from a card (number recognition). A cue of "Write number" would have Sarah write numbers (up to 40).

J, Reading A Book: The therapist engaged Sarah with the following questions: What do you see in the picture?, Who do you see in the picture?, What is happening?, What is that?, Where is (person)?, How many_____?, Tell me about the book, What is (color)?, Who is (eating)?, What is (on) the (fence)?, How does (person) feel?

K, Playing a Game: Played games and learned about turn taking.

༄

Chapter 4: Operation Kindergarten

The theatrical teacher, 1999 and 2000 (six to seven years old).
I felt so nervous on the eve before Sarah's first day of kindergarten, because on the following morning I planned to go where I typically thought no sane mother would, back to kindergarten. I felt the need to be there with Sarah until her teacher and aide understood her capabilities. The first thing that the teacher, Robyn, understood was that I was not going to leave. She probably understood that my motivation was pure, as she welcomed me warmly, quickly putting me to work; giving me things to do in between helping to build a knowledge base for endeavors in teaching Sarah. On the first day of school, as I watched Robyn and her special kind of flare for engaging her students, I felt her to be a little theatrical, a little different. She was the actor and the kids were her captive audience. She was kind of nuts in a good way. For a while, I kept those thoughts to myself. By the end of the first week of school, I noticed that she never repeated things to the kids, and she calmed many storms with a simple yet theatrical look. Sarah responded wonderfully to this. Robyn eventual told me that she learned her technique from Fred Jones. We laughed when I shared how I thought her to be a little kooky during those first days of school. What a great teacher! Sarah's classmates were great too. While she did not communicate exactly like them and acted a bit different, she showed abilities to write, read, cut, draw, and use the computer like them; sometimes better and quicker. Her classmates said, "Wow," as they watched Sarah achieve. She seemed to have the ability to tend to task as well as any kindergartener. Around Christmastime, I sent the in-home therapists an update to catch them up on Sarah.

> It has been a while since I have been in touch with all of you. I have received some nice letters and phone calls from many of you. Joy is the only way to describe my feelings with regard to Sarah's

Hello, Dr. Wells

adaptation to full time kindergarten. I hear about goings on which occur in the classroom daily. Sarah's EA, teacher, and classmates are so enthusiastic about her success in academics and peer relationship. You have all done a great thing in the life of Sarah, and I have seen the fruits of your labors on a continual basis.

Last Friday, 12/3/99, Sarah was asked by her teacher if she had anything to share for show and tell. Sarah said, "Yes." The teacher asked what she wanted to share. Sarah replied, "I want to sing." The teacher asked what Sarah would like to sing. "Polly Panda," Sarah answered and then she looked at the tape player. The teacher started playing the song and Sarah sang along perfectly. When she was finished, the entire class clapped and then Sarah took three sweeping bows. Earlier that day, there had been a chorus performance that Sarah sat through beautifully, fifty minutes long. Maybe it was just her turn to sing! On that same day, Sarah noticed that her classmate Aubrey was missing from class. She kept saying "Aubrey," with a bit of dismay. Aubrey came back to the class and Sarah said, "Aubrey," happily while dancing around. I am very happy that Sarah is forming attachments to classmates. Tomorrow I am taking them to lunch.

Sarah has accepted Robyn (teacher) and Julie (EA). At first, she had a hard time responding to questions and directives. Routine was in her favor since kindergarten is set in daily and weekly routines. Sarah became able to follow the lead of her peers depending less on verbal cues. As things progressed and days passed Sarah was able to follow directives better, respond to questions better and was proving that she understood. One day during library, the librarian had read a story about Thanksgiving. She asked Sarah what she was thankful for and Sarah responded, "Aubrey and Inna." She was thankful for her friends.

Sarah is learning to attempt conversation and experiencing success. Even her classmates are eager for Sarah to talk and interact with them. I guess you could say her classmates are her new therapists.

Ann Dunham

In the weeks before I sent the update to the in-home therapists,
I had a hard time identifying the point at which I needed to take myself
out of the school picture. One day, as some individuals encouraged me
to leave I took it so personally. I did leave, but my concerns remained,
since their ability to know or understand proper ways to interact
with Sarah was still emerging. Any lack in understanding her, created a
potential for behavior problems. Once home, I cried and rearranged
the furniture while contemplating Sarah's quirkiness. Professionals
at school simply tried to facilitate some independence for her, an
independence from the mom who would not leave! Robyn and Julie
did not try to make me leave though. They helped me to phase out
over time, eventually to the point of only having lunch with Sarah.
Then, the day finally came when Robyn stopped me while I entered
the school, on my way to yet another lunch date with Sarah. She said
that everything was fine and Sarah was not even asking for me. Robyn
suggested we go out to lunch, and so we did. The next day I got a card
from this extraordinary teacher that celebrated the fact that it only
took 45 school days to phase me out of "Operation Kindergarten",
mission complete. This was good for Sarah, but bad for the woodwork
and walls in our house, since I then started my career of inferior
decorating.

Kindergarten came and went and then it was summer. It was the first
free summer that Sarah had experienced in many years. No summer
school and very little maintenance therapy—a lot of swimming, biking,
roller blading and video games while interacting with Jeff, Jana and the
neighborhood kids.

෭

Real Time Kindergarten Notes

(Important for understanding her communicative development.)

Monday (8/30/99)
Verbal Cues *that may be useful: Sit nice, time to sit down, no
talking. Sarah is becoming used to the routine and morning
announcements. Some verbal cues that may help in having her take*

her hands off her ears: hands down, sound all gone. When Sarah wants something that it is not time for, try the following verbal cues: have to wait, first we listen to teacher. It would be helpful if we are sure that Sarah is attending to person who is speaking to her. Some eye contact needs to occur. The following cue would help to remind Sarah that she needs to attend to the teacher: Need to listen to teacher.

***Reading Time** is something that Sarah enjoys. Noticed she was really into watching the pages of the book this morning, but she had her ears covered due to the tape playing in the stereo. In the afternoon, she did not cover her ears as the teacher read without the tape.*

***Chatter:** It is always this way…when there is auditory discomfort she will use constant chatter while plugging her ears to block the noise.*

***Concerning Bell:** It had been discussed and decided that once Sarah becomes used to the routine of the school bells and announcements, she will remove her hands from her ears with the cues: sound all gone, hands down.*

***Addressing Inappropriate Behaviors:** If we chose to ignore Sarah's burping and spitting (raspberry like spitting, not at people but as a stimulatory behavior) in order that she does not get any reinforcement for those behaviors, we need to explain the situation to her classmates in a manner that they would comprehend. Something like, Sarah will watch them to know the right thing to do. They should understand that Sarah should not be doing these things. It is wrong. They should act like they didn't hear it in order to help her stop. Normally when these things happen one would say excuse me and usually wouldn't laugh.*

***Drawing a picture of herself:** She knows how to do this. I found she was confused. She was writing her name when told to draw a picture of Sarah. Instead of drawing a simple picture of herself, she wrote her name over and over. At home, I reviewed this with her and prompted by drawing a picture of a little girl in order for her to see the difference between writing a name and drawing a picture of herself. Then she drew a picture of a little girl. Maybe if she is encouraged to watch a classmate who is appropriately doing the assignment that could also be a tool for helping her along.*

Ann Dunham

Tuesday (8/31/99)
Circle Time *went so much better this morning. Sarah even sat independently without constant reminders or prompts. She is learning classroom structure and routine much quicker than I expected.*

Art: *In art, Sarah's classmates noticed how well she drew the ladybugs. She even got ahead of the teacher by putting an antenna on the ladybug head!*

Class Project: *During project of cutting gingerbread man Sarah was doing great. She could have done even better if she was not preoccupied with covering her ears while cutting and coloring.*

Quiet Time: *Will not be something Sarah will be able to do. We will maybe have to utilize the OT room for her to get some useful play.*

Misc: *"Stop" and "go" need to be reviewed with Sarah, so that when the teacher or aid tells her to "stop" she complies in a timely fashion. Walking in line needs to be enforced, reviewed. She does okay with turn taking but needs to be supervised and prompted to do right things on the playground. Don't they all? Noticed: Hand flapping, zoning in and out, distraction due to lighting, distraction due to skylights, and distraction due to blowers. Lots for Sarah to adapt to: Public address, air conditioning, demands of attending for longer periods of time, twenty classmates instead of five. Yesterday Sarah wanted to go home right before lunch period... "Want to go home," she said. She even had a couple of tantrums. Today she didn't say she wanted to go home until 1:00 p m. and never had a fit about it.*

Wednesday (9/1/99)
AM Announcements *made Sarah cry this morning. I held hands on one of her ears so she could free up her right hand to write her name five times. It is very important to me, that her abilities become apparent to her teacher, educational assistant, and classmates.*

AM Library: *I am thinking that Sarah needs to be seated in the back row, so that she and the EA have time to work and are less of a distraction. Sarah did not have her hands on her ears for library and it seems she associate the sound of the bell and PA system with* the classroom. She actually put her fingers back in her ears as she got back to the classroom.

AM Recess: When morning recess bell rang to go in Sarah ran with the rest of her classmates. She forgot to wait in the kindergarten line but she is watching and doing as her classmates.

AM Music: Went so-so. They learned about their special place to sit and sang a few songs. Sarah was spacey, but did sing a little bit.

Lunch Recess: Sarah wanted to go to the classroom before lunch recess bell sounded (end of lunch.) Not sure if it was because she wanted to get her stuff and go home, or she was anticipating the daily routine and thought recess was getting ready to be over.

Quiet Time: Not the best for Sarah!

Tantrum: Did a bit more confrontational, tantrum because she wanted to go home. Probably about 1:00 p.m. I wouldn't let the EA take her out of the room because I didn't want Sarah to associate screaming with getting her way. Getting out of the classroom may even confuse her into thinking she gets to go home. The EA and the teacher, as well as the classmates, handled it well. Yesterday there was no tantrum.

Classmates: During recess, two of Sarah's classmates repeatedly went down the slide holding hands with her. I believe she continued to seek them out for a while. In addition, a classmate tickled Sarah while she was hanging from a bar on the equipment. It is very encouraging to see the children show such great examples. One boy classmate talked about how cute she is, even after her major tantrum. When Sarah burped, two of her classmates looked backed disapprovingly and I am glad. No classmate has even laughed or given any reinforcement for inappropriate behaviors. These children are doing an excellent job of attending to their teacher and not allowing Sarah's few episodes to rule the day!

Thursday (9/2/99)

AM Announcements: Some discomfort, but no crying. She put her fingers in her ears hindering her ability to perform classroom activities: Coloring with markers, circle time dancing and Who Stole the Cookie?

Ann Dunham

AM Stations: I placed my hands on Sarah's ears to free up her hands for completing tasks. Played Candyland with a classmate. Used hand over hand to help Sarah stay on task here and there. Sarah finished the game and actually won. Her classmate was a good sport and wanted very much to help. She did puzzles quickly, except for Little Bo Peep puzzle that was a harder. Sometimes Sarah looks at only the shape or only the color, instead of looking at shape and color to fit the piece. It would be okay to cue her with: look at the color, look at the shape. Cutting and drawing on line were both easy. No problem.

AM Circle Time: Sarah sat for it well, with a little chatter and I don't think she screamed. Still, the biggest problem was her fingers in her ears. That hinders her ability to participate in some fun activities.

AM Recess: Sarah ran to the line to wait and go in.

Lunch: She is sitting nicely to eat, but I still don't think you can count on her to stay in her seat when one is not looking. I think she will head straight for the door and to the playground without being excused first.

Lunch Recess: Kids are curious about Sarah. One told me her mom had a brother like that. Sarah sat on the slide with one girl, held her hand, waited for another girl to sit, held her hand and they all went down the slide together…smiling.

PM Quiet Time: Went well because they watched Richard Scarey, Gingerbread Man video. When the counselor came in to talk with the kids Sarah was not ready to sit and listen, that was right after quiet time.

Art: Sarah did great and even was ahead of the teacher.

PM Recess: Went well except she tried to make a break for it, running for my car when she thought we weren't looking. She made it to my car about the same time that I caught up with her. She thought the whole thing was funny.

Traffic Safety: Sarah dug that end of the day project. Cutting, using glue and writing…all things she is great at doing.

Hello, Dr. Wells

Friday (9/3/99)
AM: *Sarah did well during story time. The Enormous Watermelon was a neat book. Sarah said that she liked it. When the teacher brought out a real watermelon, Sarah had a hard time staying away from it and kept getting out of her circle spot. She made it a point to tell her EA that she wanted me by saying, "Sit with Mom." When we did not comply, she had a tantrum. Sarah called the EA by name but I can't remember under what circumstance it occurred. In the past she has always learned first names of teachers and therapist, so she called the EA Julie. If that is not okay, we might try "Ms. Julie." Sarah likes the Freeze song and understands the idea of stopping immediately. If saying "stop" hasn't been effective maybe we can try "freeze" under some circumstances. Then she would probably comply because she associates freeze with fun.*
AM Gym: *Sarah did well with supervision. She will get better with staying on task concerning participation in PE. I took Sarah home at lunchtime to assure finishing a wonderful first week on a positive note. I wanted to reward her and it was important to put the reward in place before she actually started asking to, "Go home." She tends to start asking after lunch.*

Tuesday (9/7/99) and Wednesday (9/8/99)
Predictability is Sarah's friend: *Sarah is learning the routine nicely. Circle time is better each day. Recess is her favorite. Lunch is enjoyable for her. We have not heard "Want to go home" from Sarah nearly as frequently as we did last week.*
Teacher and EA: *Sarah responds very nicely to Robyn. Sarah has responded to Julie's authority more and more each day. It is hard for Julie because I am in the class, and so Sarah pulls the "I want Mom" thing. It has been less frequent this week.*
Behaviors: *Sarah has almost stopped the burping and other noises that are unacceptable. She has been doing a bit of gibberish, but it is not near as loud or as frequent as I expected it to be.*
Speech: *Sarah did nicely in speech with both therapists.*
Phasing Mom out: *Sarah has seen me leave the class and specials and has not displayed as much resistance to my leaving*

as I expected. She gave Julie a bit of a run for her money when I left during art, but Julie was able to get Sarah back on task quickly. Sarah did not want to leave art until I came back and so she cried when they left art. She stopped crying the minute she saw that I was in the kindergarten room. She does not care when I leave the classroom to make copies or whatever else.

Monday (9/13/99)
Phasing Mom out: Left during morning specials. I wanted to take an anniversary gift to Steve's work. Sarah did pretty well. It was time to start phasing my constant presence down anyway. Came back during lunchtime and spent the rest of the day in the kindergarten room.

Tuesday (9/14/99) & Wednesday (9/15/99)
Spent most of both days in kindergarten room, but did not go to specials.

Thursday (9/16/99) & Friday (9/17/99)
Brought Sarah in the morning, came for lunch and left after lunch recess. I came back after her lasts recess of the day. She began to get anxious if she did not see me while she was in the OT room after last recess.

Monday (9/20/99)
Had a great day but continues to get anxious in the last part of the school day. I will just go spend lunchtime with Sarah. I will slowly come later and later after her last recess to pick her up.
School Counselor: The school counselor directed a question to Sarah, "Sarah, do you want to sit in front?" Sarah responded, "Yes." Then she moved up in front and sat next to Inna. Inna was excited that Sarah had picked her.
Interactions: Also, there was a good interaction with other kids during recess to do with holding hands going down the slide. As we were walking to the car after school today, a classmate said, "Goodbye." to Sarah. Sarah responded with, "Goodbye!"

Hello, Dr. Wells

Wednesday (9/22/99)
Sarah does fine while I am gone. I still will go for lunch as it breaks up the long day. She sat with kids during quiet time as they watched a video. I should probably wait until 2:30 tomorrow to pick up.

Monday (9/27/99)
Sarah does great when I am gone except if she doesn't see me during the routine times that have currently been established: Right before lunch and right after last recess. I will slowly phase out the lunch routine as I think Sarah may attempt to communicate with her peers if I wasn't there. I will still come after recess for a while.
***Art Teacher:** Last week, Peg came up to me to tell me how much she enjoys Sarah...*
***Speech:** Last week, the speech gal told me that Sarah outsmarted the Earobics computer game by going into the options to get out of the hard stuff!*
***Dinner:** Took kids out to dinner after school. We ordered drinks and then Sarah threw up all over me. Wow did that take me by surprise. That is the first time she has thrown up since she had her surgery for pyloric stenosis when she was three weeks old.*

Tuesday (9/28/99)
Let Sarah go to school for the morning, then took her home after lunch as she still did not seem herself. She stayed home and watched Veggie Tales.

Wednesday (9/29/99)
Sarah does fine when I am not at school. She still expects me during lunch. She had a major hissy fit, tantrum during lunch and everybody in the lunchroom knew that she wanted "Candy", and she wanted to "Go to the playground." She did not get either because she was screaming. She sat where kids who are misbehaving are made to sit and she did not get to go out for recess. From now on only healthy choices of food for lunch so that candy is not an option.
***Classmates:** Aubrey asked me why I didn't bring Sarah's Rugrats lunch box. I had to tell her that it was still in my car and it was dirty so we packed a different one. I don't think Aubrey approved. Several*

classmates noticed right away that Sarah had a different backpack one day. Guess that is also not acceptable. When I leave, classmates ask me where I am going and when I will be back. When I do get back, they inform me on how Sarah did while I was gone; and she has been doing great! Alex came up to me to say that Sarah has been doing so well when I am gone. No screaming, no burping. Alex felt that they were doing a great job teaching Sarah...and I agree. These kids are not going to let her get away with anything. They are awesome.

Thursday (9/30/99)
She stayed home sick. She had a high fever and slept most of the morning. She looked at me and said, "I love you," and I told her that I loved her right back. Got to love those spontaneous displays of affection. This was the first verbal display I have ever gotten.

Friday (10/1/99)
Sarah got to stay home again today...but I do think her fever broke. She keeps yelling for fries.

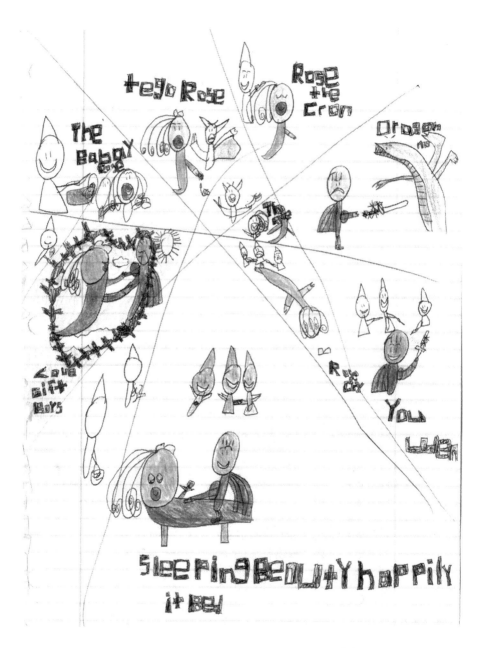

Illustrated by Sarah in 1999

Chapter 5: Singing, Dancing Ladybugs

Decline in adaptability, 2000 and 2001 (seven to eight years old). In no time, first grade started. Sarah had the same dedicated educational assistant (EA), and her first grade teacher was Carol. Sarah told me to go home on the first day of school, a firmly set routine from kindergarten. I drop her off. I pick her up. Routine, routine, it is always the routine! Fortunately, Carol acquainted herself with Sarah a couple of years earlier due to time spent in her preschool room, learning much about her educative process and ability. That was a good thing seeing as Sarah literally kicked me out of the classroom! As first grade ensued, Sarah continued to model her classmates' appropriate behavior at times. Yet the behaviors that set her apart remained present on a daily basis in the classroom. The auditory sensitivity did not magically disappear. The announcements were still bothersome and the teachers encouraged Sarah to deal with the discomfort in different ways.

In kindergarten, Sarah seemed to do well with understanding expectations through watching others for cues. That coupled with the highly defined routines of the days and weeks seemed to offer a lot of success. Instructions were very succinct in kindergarten, thus she was more apt to be able to follow them. First grade proved to be different. Since Sarah continued to have struggles with receptive and expressive communication, complete integration in the regular classroom made less sense as the school year progressed. From a behavioral perspective, I related her worsening in performance to the facts that the language load from the teacher became necessarily larger, and the requirement of students needing to sit and attend for longer durations grew. For Sarah, it certainly became a time for some screaming. There were times in the past when she utilized screaming, and notes from in-home therapy confirm that. Kindergarten did not experience screaming to near the degree that first grade was, to my knowledge. Carol became concerned enough to make the principal aware of the episodes, in case of any parent complaints. A nurse, who happened to be in the classroom during one episode, felt that Sarah needed to be on something. We never used medication as intervention because the behavioral approach seemed to be working, at least from our home perspective.

First grade realized wonderful things too, my favorite being Sarah's participation in a school musical. She liked being a ladybug along with some of her classmates. They sang and danced during their special time in the performance. The audience never noticed the *different* child in that group of singing, dancing ladybugs. Such a joy! Carol and Julie made that happen. They masterfully finagled it so that Sarah had that part and the opportunity to participate in something grand with her typical peers! Funny thing being, the decision to include her in the musical had bothered some. Nevertheless, on that night when all went well with the performance, those disturbed by Carol and Julie's advocacy bragged on Sarah's accomplishment, even taking some credit for it. Sarah also successfully participated in reading to some residents at a care facility by her school, which really thrilled Carol. The first grade year evidenced two educators who assumed huge responsibility.

Toward the end of first grade, Sarah's three year evaluation transpired. After assessment by an educator, psychologist, and speech therapist, we met. That meeting brought me face to face with the fact that the educative processes we had involved Sarah in had taken her far, but also created a problem for the system in which we placed her. My continuing focus on the idea that she might become more like her typical peers by being around them all of the time, became a burdensome problem, not easily shouldered. Full integration with typical peers in a typical classroom might have actually contributed to bad patterns of behavior for Sarah, since she did not thrive in the classroom and experienced frustration. While being afraid that time in resource would take away from Sarah, I ignored the possibility that new learning might transpire there. My hope's alignment fell within a limited scope of how the school journey must transpire, representing hope in a tunnel instead of hope on the horizon. Since the glimmers that edified the grand idea of integration remained present to some degree, I wanted full integration to work even as it really did not work. What I mean by glimmer is the potential factor that Sarah showed here and there in the regular classroom. What I mean by grand idea is the hope that with each year she might begin to become more and more like her normal peers in form and function, just by being around them. Second grade shook my glimmers and grand ideas.

An educational assessment report provided such good information on Sarah's performance in first grade.

> *EDUCATIONAL ASSESSMENT REPORT DATE OF REPORT: 5-15-01 STUDENT: Sarah (8 yrs)*
>
> *Test Observations: ... Sarah is a first grade student.... She was referred to the autism evaluation team for a three-year reevaluation. She currently receives speech language services and assistance in the classroom with an educational assistant. The evaluation team consisted of a school psychologist, a speech therapist, and an educator. This report reflects the testing and observations completed by the educator. Assessments were given to assess Sarah's current level of achievement in academic skill areas. Observations were completed (at school) in her first grade classroom, art class, recess, lunch and transitions in the school.*
>
> *Sarah's teacher and educative assistant prepared her for the change in schedule the day of testing by explaining to her who she would be working with, when it would happen and where we would be working. Sarah transitioned to the conference room without showing stress. While walking to the conference room, she answered a few social questions. Sarah sat nicely throughout most of the testing session. When test questions became more challenging Sarah asked to go back to her classroom by saying "time to go", "one more time" and "OK, time to stop" She got out of her chair*

twice and started to open the door but sat back down with simple verbal redirection. She was very cooperative and gave effort to each question.

Items for the assessment were presented in two formats. In the first test session, the Test of Early Reading Ability (TERA-2) and Test of Early Written Language (TEWL-2) were given in typical standardized administration. In the second session, items missed during the first test session were given in a visual, more structured format that allowed Sarah to point or write as opposed to verbally answering questions. The Test of Early Mathematics Ability (TEMA-2) was also given at this time. It was very frustrating for her when she did not understand the language of the test questions, so items involving rote understanding were intermixed with items requiring more language processing to limit frustration. Given this format, Sarah was able to demonstrate understanding of more test concepts than in the first session. The results of these tests should be compared with Sarah's daily classroom performance to best understand her achievement in school. Sarah's teacher and this evaluator both agree that the standardized testing is most likely a low estimate of Sarah's true academic skills. Her knowledge is difficult to assess due to her difficulties in language.

SUMMARY OF ASSESSMENT RESULTS AS THEY RELATE TO EDUCATIONAL PLANNING
...In this testing session the student displayed the ability to (strengths):
— Read beginning sight words, sentences, and short stories.
— Use letter sound knowledge to discriminate between words and read words.
— Use sight word memory and letter sound knowledge to phonetically write words and dictate sentences.
— Identify punctuation marks (pointing) upon request (period, question mark).
— Demonstrates an emerging understanding of when to use periods and question marks.

– Draw detailed sequenced pictures to express ideas and retell stories.
– Rote count past 50 without errors or prompts.
– Accurately count sets of objects to 20 and write how many.
– Identify and write single and double digit numerals.
– Demonstrates emerging understanding of addition concepts using manipulatives.
In this testing session the student did not display the ability to (needs):
– Demonstrate consistent understanding and use of spaces in between words (this is emerging).
– Categorize words (find words that go together and words that don't belong).
– Fill in words to finish stories or poems.
– Verbally answer questions to demonstrate understanding of story concepts.
– Write stories without prompts to start sentences and structure ideas.
– Independently use correct punctuation and capitalize in writing.
– Perform addition problems without prompts and assistance to organize manipulatives.
– Demonstrate memorization of addition facts.
– Count out a given set of objects consistently (ex: give me 17 blocks).
– Consistently demonstrate understanding of more and less and number line relationships.

THE CHILDHOOD AUTISM RATING SCALE – CARS
…The following rating reports are based on observations by this special education evaluator. Multiple observations were conducted in Sarah's classroom, testing sessions, art class, recess, and lunch. The total rating score using the CARS from this evaluator is 42. Areas receiving a score of 3 or higher (moderate to moderate/severe concern) included relating to people, imitation, emotional response, body use, adaptation to change, visual response, listening response, verbal communication, nonverbal communication, activity level and general impressions.

Hello, Dr. Wells

LEADING LUNCH COUNT & CALENDAR

During the observations in the first grade classroom, Sarah's performance and behavior varied. Her teacher reports that Sarah is compliant most of the time. The times she has difficulties are usually related to a schedule change or explainable incident. Sarah had a very successful experience leading her class in the morning routine. She assisted the teacher by tallying students eating hot lunch or cold lunch during roll call. She listened and wrote tally marks for student responses needing only a few cues from her education assistant. The classroom routine is to double check the lunch count by asking the kids to stand and counting heads. Her teacher prompted her with a model sentence and Sarah repeated the sentence quietly. She chose a friend to walk to the office with her to deliver the lunch count. Sarah was very cooperative and successful in this activity, although she gave very little visual attention to her classmate. Sarah also led the class in the morning calendar and weather routine. Leading in this activity was more challenging for her. Sarah's teacher maintained high expectations for her to perform throughout this activity, but also modified the directions to make it more successful (using one and two word commands and pointing to visual cues when she was frustrated). Sarah used a pointer, counters with manipulatives to count the days in school, complete the calendar and explore patterns. When Sarah was confused or frustrated, she voiced her refusals and frustrations by screaming.

JOURNALING

Sarah has a journal in which she expresses her thoughts and ideas visually with pictures and with words and short phrases to label the item. Her pictures are quite fascinating and colorful. She draws eyes, eyebrows and mouths on people that express different emotions (happiness, anger, sleepiness, excitement). Her visual stories are sequenced and detailed. Sarah uses a variety of letter writing styles, almost like computer font. Given prompts to start sentences and fill in missing words, Sarah also writes stories with her teacher and educational assistant. The teacher has Sarah read and present her stories to her classmates. This is a great opportunity for Sarah to

Ann Dunham

interact with her friends and an opportunity for them to see her creativity. During math class, Sarah uses manipulatives to count out addition problems on a worksheet. Sarah cooperated with completing the worksheets, but needed quite a bit of assistance from her education assistant to organize the manipulatives and maintain attention. Sarah was focused on wanting the computer at that time.

SCIENCE

During a large group science activity at the end of the day, Sarah had more difficulty managing her behavior. When requested to sit to listen to a book with her class, Sarah screamed repeatedly and lay on the floor. She requested over and over to use the computer by saying, "Time for computer, Mom coming soon". Her assistant tried several redirections (having her sit in a chair, using visual cue to sit nice) unsuccessfully. Eventually she needed to be removed from the room (*walked out, not carried out). Sitting on the floor in the hallway, Sarah continued to scream, engaging in repetitive motor movements and repeated phrases over and over. Given time to calm herself, Sarah was given the choice to return to the room to "sit nice". She refused the first couple of times, but then chose to go back. Her EA calmly led Sarah to the activity area and guided her to rejoin the group. Shortly thereafter the students moved to their desk to complete a butterfly activity. Sarah enjoyed this and completed the activity without displaying inappropriate behaviors.

ART

The art class observed was a very successful time for Sarah. The class was structured alternating large group demonstrations with time for independent drawing. During the demonstrations, the art teacher sat next to Sarah to help her attend (and had) the class gather around Sarah's group table. This was an effective strategy in that Sarah did not have to get up to transition and she had a "front row seat" to watch the demonstration. When Sarah was not attending, her EA prompted her quietly to watch and listen. Sarah independently completed the drawing activity exactly as demonstrated. Because she worked quickly, her EA gave her

75

a drawing paper to keep appropriately busy while waiting for classmates to catch up. Sarah engaged in quiet self talk while drawing. She was not distracting to her classmates.

RECOMMENDATIONS:
SITTING FOR TOO LONG AND VERBAL vs. VISUAL
The amount of time expected to sit in one place and listen to verbal presentation (listening books, directions, teacher demonstrations) increases as students move up through elementary grades. Sarah learns and demonstrates understanding most effectively with visual, hands on tasks. She does very well with concrete tasks that are more rote in nature and struggles with abstract concepts and language processing concepts. Her team may want to consider building her schedule to break up the long periods of sitting with small group opportunities to work on her individual academic needs. Sarah is making gains in reading, writing and math; unfortunately standardized tests and regular classroom curriculum for these academic areas include the need to process a lot of verbal language. She will need her curriculum adapted in two ways. The presentation of material will need to be made quite visual and delivered in sequential rote manner so that Sarah has repeated opportunities to learn and retain concepts. The method in which Sarah is expected to demonstrate understanding of concepts will also need to be modified. Sarah is very artistic and expressive in her pictures. She currently draws detailed pictures with a sequence to retell a story, labeling the pictures with words and phrases. In testing, Sarah's responses were more accurate and she was less stressed when she was allowed to point to answers (for multiple choices), write answers, or draw pictures to represent the answers.

SCREAMING
To voice her refusals and frustrations Sarah screams. She needs to have a more appropriate way to voice her refusals and frustrations. Her team has recently addressed the behavior by using visual cards to help her better understand expectations (card showing picture and words to sit nice, stop screaming, time out). These cards are great visual cues of expectations. Using a daily visual schedule

may also help Sarah better understand changes that happen. She may have difficulty truly understanding changes if they are only presented verbally. Schedules, like personal calendars we all keep and rely on, help reduce stress. We don't have to worry about surprises or understanding schedule changes if we show her a schedule that shows what is going to happen (and when) each day. She would need access to the schedule throughout the day so that she can remind herself of upcoming events. She could even participate in making schedule changes by crossing out activities that won't happen and writing in special events (i.e., assembly today). The visual schedule can be used to help monitor her behavior. When she is determined to use the computer, her schedule could show when computer time is available...

Brenda, Autism Evaluation Team Educator

❧

Hello, Dr. Wells

Illustrated by Sarah

Chapter 6: Buying an Island

Decline and regression, 2001 &2002 (eight and nine years old). Summer reflections about Sarah's school experience throughout first grade caused me to consider extensively, her placement for the upcoming second grade year. When Sarah's receptive communicative function presented challenges in kindergarten and first grade, staff utilized the already established communicative strengths, the many phrases that had been discernable to her throughout her earliest years. Some of those are in *Kindergarten Notes*. Sarah did not have a consistent ability to process heavy language loads. When necessary, the teachers presented classroom lessons creatively in order to override her lack in typical language comprehension. The teachers learned Sarah's lingo, and the sequential and concrete way that her mind worked. They sequenced delivery of instructions and behavior expectations by first, then, next, since that gave Sarah a higher probability for experiencing success. Speaking "Sarah" meant knowing the cues that she understood and even more so, it seemed to mean one must know her very psyche. In order for Sarah to learn among her typical peers, the teachers learned a somewhat complicated behavioral and psychological dance. That dance developed some edginess about halfway through first grade. My behavioral perspective of that time blamed the increase in language load for instruction, less concrete teaching concepts, and the necessity for Sarah to understand abstract thought processes.

My ongoing considerations about Sarah's placement continued to test the idea that second grade would be ready for her. That being said, autism has already created her lack of readiness, and the school mandate is that of dealing with it, each and every year. The unanswerable questions nagged at me. How could she experience academic growth in the regular classroom? How could she receive benefit from exposure to typical peers if she was not in the regular classroom? How much had being in the regular classroom helped—especially given the time, energy, and sacrifice imparted by the students and teachers? Sarah lived every day with two typical kids and that did not cause her to be more like them. With so many questions swimming in my mind, I felt that I failed Sarah, and that caused an ongoing melancholy; during which, I occasionally dreamed aloud to Steve. I told him to make enough money to buy a small island somewhere for us to live, where the only people allowed would be those who spoke Sarah, and they could not bring a public address system either. Since we did not buy an island, our house became an island and the pool in our backyard became her ocean.

Ann Dunham

Steve & Sarah

Hello, Dr. Wells

Sarah spent glorious days swimming in the pool, eating popcorn, and romping with Jeff, Jana, and some of the neighborhood kids. She had a free and unstructured summer, and developed a real problem with screaming. During the previous school year, she reserved the behavior for intermittent use. With school out for the summer, the screaming reared its head at home over many identifiable causes, but it also happened over nothing. She also started to lament, "No. Help! Momma. Dad. Help!" when she was frustrated, doing so even when I was the one with her. When she did this in public, I would get some very strange looks. I kept waiting for the day when the police would need to be convinced that she was indeed my child, and I was not a kidnapper. I ignored her screaming for a long few weeks, and it seemed as if I won the battle because she stopped her utilization of screaming. Unfortunately, I forgot that behaviors represent a war in Sarah's case, and I had yet to identify all of the enemies. The idea that the screaming stopped due to lack of reinforcement comforted me, and I did not entertain the notion that screaming can come for nonsensical reasons, and from places where a trigger is hard to identify.

My perception that I helped Sarah past her behavior of screaming at home gave relief, but I remained anxious about her overall learning process, especially the behavioral aspects. Keeping her with Julie for a third school year was going to continue fostering a burdensome dependence on one individual. The same-aide scenario seemed to create a pseudo mom for school. I made the decision that Sarah needed to have a different aide for her second grade year. While the concept was right, the prospect was frightening, and it was like pulling the rug right out from under Sarah.

I tried reacquainting Sarah to the school environment, on and off, for about a week before second grade was to start. She happily met her newest teacher, but she did not have a good reaction to being back in the school environment. It looked like total sensory overload—same suspects: Air conditioner blowers, lighting, and the PA system. While always a challenge, her reactions seemed stronger and more negative than at the start of first grade when she had similarly been away all summer. Sarah's reaction perplexed me. Soon enough, the first day of school arrived. As Sarah sat at her desk, she suffered through morning announcements. Observing her extreme discomfort made me sad, and as I watched my daughter, the kids who had followed through the grades watched too. They asked me what was wrong and said that Sarah was not acting like herself. All this and Sarah was telling me to go home. Routine, routine, it is always the routine.

The person that the school hired and trained specifically for Sarah failed to show up, and that created a huge problem. Whoever worked with Sarah needed to know the cues that she understood. They needed to speak "Sarah". As the days passed, my concern increased, because not only were Sarah's classmates worried; staff and even some parents were approaching me and asking what was wrong with Sarah. Nobody understood her lack of ability to engage in activities and tasks that previously proved successful for her. One day, I watched a substitute EA treat Sarah as if she had no ability at all. She grabbed Sarah's crayons out and colored for her! Sarah did not understand the sub and became quite agitated. It was not the sub's fault, since she did not know that Sarah's comprehension suffered under heavier language loads. During those weeks of school, the only conclusion that explained Sarah's lack of performance was that she was performing according to expectations; they were not even close to being high. However, she was not demonstrating her abilities to the new teachers either. How could the teachers know her level of performance, if she rarely displayed it? Much adjustment became necessary.

In an effort to try to get the overall system to understand Sarah and her previous ability to perform so well in plays, in kindergarten, and in some of first grade, I became the memo-writing mom. I needed to convince everyone who worked with Sarah that she did have some good skills. In one memo, I wanted to show them that they should not overload her with excess language.

Hello, Dr. Wells

MEMO TO TEACHERS
Hello, Just wanted to share some communication exchanges that
Sarah engaged in today.
Ann – "Sarah, it is time to get Jeffrey."
Sarah – "Jeffrey, then McDonald's?"
Ann – "No. No McDonald's. Let's get Jeff."
Sarah – "First Jeffrey, then McDonald's."
Ann – "Okay, McDonald's."
In the car:
Sarah – "McDonald's?"(I knew she was shooting for McDonald's
before Jeffrey.)
Ann – "No. First Jeffrey, then McDonald's."
Sarah – "No. First McDonald's then Jeffrey."
Ann – "Okay. First McDonald's, then Jeffrey."
Sarah – "Chicken, french fries and soda?"
Ann – "Yes. Chicken, french fries and soda."
Also in car:
I spilled some coke on my legs while driving. I asked Sarah for a
napkin ("Give me a napkin.") and then she handed me two from
her happy meal bag. She was sitting in the back seat. So nothing
would have clued her in to what I needed except for my verbal
request.

I also wrote an extensive report of Sarah's educative history and
provided it to everyone who worked with her. To some I knew it
would just be a lot of talk from a denial mom. (Denial mom was an
unfortunate phrase used by some who work with kids like Sarah.) I
did not care about what *everyone* thought, and I just hoped that a *few*
would read it and grow in their understanding of Sarah. A few did.

Into the first couple of months of second grade, everyone understood
that there needed to be an intervention for Sarah's utilization
of screaming. It was so disappointing; I had thought her use of
screaming had disappeared over the summer. The school tried some
interventions that did not result in improvement, so I requested
intervention by a well-respected behavioral specialist. Bruce came
and observed, and then wrote up a Behavior Intervention Plan

(BIP) with all the right elements for extinguishing the screaming behavior—ignore, redirect, and do not reward for her for the screaming, especially by removing her from the classroom. A good plan in theory, but it did not work in the regular education classroom, and so modification of the BIP resulted in lessening the effect of screaming on the other students.

A lot of quality time happened for Sarah in the resource room during her second grade year. She displayed ability to function in the regular education room at times throughout the school day. As far as I knew, during past school years, she participated well in art, gym, and computer with her more typical peers. Her ability to participate in those specials really changed in second grade, as her behaviors just started getting the better of her. I did not attribute her decline in performance to lack of trying on the instructors' part, because I witnessed their perseverance while trying to teach Sarah, and their joy in reporting the good days.

- *Classroom Journal Entries*
  (1/8/02) Hi Ann. Art class was awesome on Tuesday, Jan 8! Sarah seemed so happy. We started a new project; I gave directions and demonstrations at Sarah's table for some steps and at the board for others. She handled the transitions very well! I have been working on having Sarah and I saying goodbye to each other at the end of class. Tuesday as she passed by me, I said, "Goodbye Sarah," and she said goodbye to me without a prompt! Peg (art)
- *(1/14/02) Ann. She is really having some great days. I started her on subtraction and she is doing great. We have also been working on counting money using dimes, nickels and pennies. We are also still practicing addition. I am hoping to be able to mix subtraction and addition on one page. So Sarah will need to watch the signs. Today she read Annie and the Wild Animals by Jan Brett. We will re read it tomorrow and try taking the AR test! Sue (teacher)*
- *(1/17/02) Today in resource, Sarah played a computer game with Breanna. It was a math game. A few times when Breanna*

didn't know the answer Sarah would point to the numbers she should use. I think it really shows her math progress. The problems were like: 7 - ___ = 5, or 5 + ___ = 9. Neat to see. Becca (educational assistant)

- *(1/31/02) Classroom journal entry: Ann. Science was a great experience for Sarah today. We were mixing colored water to get the colors of the spectrum. She was excited about the experiment and followed the lesson. Sarah also finished a social studies project and earned free computer time with Christina. The snow was a real thrill; she enjoyed her recess time very much and spent some time playing with several other children. It has been a good week for Sarah. She has worked hard and had appropriate behavior skills in room 201. Hopefully the settling of the schedule will be a real benefit for Sarah. Keep in touch. Karen (teacher)*

In the years that would follow, I engaged in many reflections about second grade. During second grade, I became aware of the fact that Sarah turned out of the ordinary behavioral outburst into ritualistic events. That is to say, she re-enacted behavioral outburst to perfection, thinking that she must do so as part of an ongoing repertoire. What follows are a couple explanations of what I mean by this. I kept track of the reports on Sarah's outburst and identified that if she had an outburst during Art on Thursday for whatever reason, she would repeat with a pretty exact reenactment the outburst on the very next Thursday, during Art again. Even with the initial reason (trigger) for the very first event absent. She engaged in similar behavior in her earliest years and I just dealt with it by coaching Sarah. The first time that I recall being witness to her penchant for doing so, we had been rollerblading. She was perhaps six years old. She had a gnarly wreck at a certain spot on the path. She cried for a while, but then we continued to skate. The next day when we went rollerblading, I watched as she deliberately made herself have the same wreck in the same spot. It was a re-enactment done to absolute perfection. I looked at her and was so surprised. I said something like, "Oh! Sarah, you do not have to do that. You don't have to wreck every time we take this turn." The next time that we went rollerblading, I made sure to be right beside her when we got to that spot, holding her hand so that she did not wreck. She never wrecked there again. The fact that she utilized her memories in this fashion was, and continues to be, fascinating to me. Therefore, for all the second grade teachers, I explained that Sarah needed redirection to stop the outburst. I told them it might take changing up her schedule sometimes, so that she was not in art at exactly that time. She needed involvement in some different activity so that no trigger or association reminded her of the initial episode, or even the reenacted episodes. If they did this, the behavior patterns might extinguish. For Sarah there needed to be a whole lot of something new under the sun! During this period, I wondered about time-of-day triggers for behaviors that had initially surfaced due to the times of day when the obnoxious PA system blared. On holidays, or weekdays of no school, she exhibited agitation and covered her ears at exactly the time that the school utilized the PA system in the morning and afternoon. The defensiveness and agitation occurred even with the PA (stimulus) absent, and time of day as the only trigger.

Chapter 7: Milk and Cookie Rats

Planning second In-home program, 2002 and 2003 (nine to ten years old). Retrospectively, contemplation turned into some contentions with the school district, starting with the troubles that surfaced in second grade. I felt that the reason for Sarah's struggles was that the district did not have a handle on best practices that were complimentary to the teaching that helped her in her earliest years. I became very vocal with regard to thoughts on teacher training and next steps for Sarah. Letters to the editor and notifications to politicians ensued. The published letters to the editor contained about the fanciest talk imaginable. The contact with the politicians resulted in conversations back and forth with both offices. Then I engaged in due process with the school district. Many times during Sarah's second grade year, it seemed as if teachers and therapists started going out of their way to walk down a different hall when they saw me. Perhaps I was being paranoid, but I was the troublemaker. Right or wrong that was the way I was.

Overall, her third grade year started on a much more successful note than her second grade year. The teachers kept on track in their efforts to reach and teach her. The most fascinating thing I remember about third grade is when Sarah illustrated a science project to do with Milk and Cookie, the rats. The regular education teacher had two rats in the classroom and the kids fed healthy food to one and not so healthy food to the other. The students were very involved with feeding the rats and observing the results of their differing diets. Sarah illustrated the research perfectly, as one sequences and illustrates a comic strip. I had no knowledge of the rats in the classroom until I showed the illustrations to Sarah's EA and she told me about the rats! We both became very excited to see how much she had taken in about Milk and Cookie.

Illustrated by Sarah

Sarah suffered from interstitial cystitis (IC) during this year. At first, everyone but one family practice doctor and I felt it was obsessive compulsive disorder. Some teachers tried to intervene from a more behavioral perspective, with regard to Sarah's discomfort and need to visit the bathroom too frequently. To me, that simply implied that they did not believe a health issue caused her discomfort. Since the problem manifested at night and kept her awake, I knew this particular problem did not relate to obsessive compulsive. I did allow a trial of Paxil since the developmental doctor was insistent that the problem was obsessive compulsive, but it did not stop the frequent trips to the bathroom. Additionally, as we titrated up to full dose the Paxil caused Sarah to become violent, thus I discontinued it. During this same period, an urologist understood Sarah's problem, using a scope to see her cracked and bleeding bladder. Hers was one of the worst cases the doctor had ever seen. Detrol alleviated the bladder spasms, and Sarah stopped going to the bathroom all of the time. I have since wondered if Sarah had this IC problem all of her life since she would engage in the behavior of squeezing her legs together with great force from a very young age. All along, I thought it to be a stimulatory behavior, but relating the behavior to bladder spasms is not too far of a reach.

Sarah's screaming remained present during third grade, so I continued to search for ways to extinguish it. I discovered an interesting approach by one intervention and gave it a try. It involved input from her peers. Comments from a couple of them were probably the most beautiful thing I saw from third grade. This is the one and only survey from third grade because I think the teacher got in trouble for letting me do it!

If Sarah screams...
- *Then it hurts my ears...so if she makes it through a science class she gets a reward.*
- *Then it hurts my ears.*
- ***I worry about her...so promise her something!***
- *Then it distracts me during work...if Sarah screams she has to go in the hall, when she is quiet she will get an award.*

- *Then it gives me a headache...so if she doesn't be noisy she can pick an award.*
- *Then I get a headache...so if Sarah gets through class without screaming she will get a pump of skittles.*
- *Then it makes me sad and hurts my ears...so chose a reward!*
- *Then it keeps me from learning and concentrating...so when she gets through a class she can have a pump full of skittles.*
- *Then it distracts me...so Sarah should quit! If Sarah makes it through a class she can have a reward.*
- **I don't care. I have handled it for two years! So Sarah should try and be patient. For one thing I really don't care when she screams because I want a kid like Sarah.**
- **Then I feel bad because I can't help Sarah...so can you let Sarah sit by me in a chair because I sit in a chair. Sarah can chose a reward if she can get through a class without screaming. Rewards: skittles, listen to books, pencil, stickers.**
- *Then it distracts me...so she should get a reward for not screaming.*
- *Then I am worried...so if she makes it through one class she will get a pump of skittles.*
- *Then it gives me a little headache...*
- **I don't care, but it makes me worry...so be patient.**
- *Then it gives me a headache...so if she makes it through science she could pick what she wants to do after.*

I shared the responses with Sarah. She comprehended enough, and she did not want to see. The kids' responses opened my eyes. Seeing the effects of her screaming made me decide to start actively planning for another in-home program. We needed to teach Sarah the hard stuff at home, where if she screamed every now and then it would not matter. In her earliest years, pre teaching concepts at home and then allowing her to show what she learned at school seemed to work really well. I became tired of the advocating I attempted through due process, because I needed to settle a couple of things about Sarah. Had she regressed? Was she capable of learning more? Gone were my fancy talking arguments. It was time to make what I thought could happen, happen at home. The strong beliefs I held about Sarah's knowledge and learning needed a platform for hands on expression, so that those beliefs became acts, not just ideas. In order to figure out if Sarah experienced ongoing regression, I asked for help from a specialist that Sarah's developmental doctor recommended. The specialist reviewed testing scores from throughout placement in the public school system. This person actually worked for the district in prior years.

EDUCATIONAL ASSESSMENT
(Assessment was facilitated by) sequencing Sarah's progress not only by test scores, (but also) by behaviors and goals for the years that she has been in school. I did take the scores starting February 1996 to October 2002, and tried to put them in a chronological sequence to evaluate if progress has been demonstrated by the use of standard scores.

An example of the scores would indicate that in February 1996, Sarah was functioning at about 35 percent of her chronological age. In October 1998, she was functioning at about 75 percent of chronological age using ratio percentage. (*We had begun an hour-intensive teaching program in our home in April of 1997...so that had been running about one and a half years when Sarah was tested again in October 1998.)

On the Peabody Picture Vocabulary Test and Expressive One-Word Test in October 1998, standard scores were 70 below 55 respectively. In May 2001, the Peabody Picture Vocabulary Test standard test score was 49 and the Expressive One – Word was 66, which does indicate a downward trend in scores.

On the Vineland Adaptive Behavior Scale, scores from 1996 have gone from 68 composite in 1998 to a composite of approximately 50 in 2001, indicating again a decline in scores.

The Leiter scale was administered and I am not sure that the same form was administered each time, therefore reporting the standard scores are not necessarily appropriate. However in 1996, it was 89, the brief form in 1998 was 97, and May 2001, the score was 77.

On the KABC, tests were administered in 1996 and 2001. Scores in 1996 were sequential 78, simultaneous 60, and composite of 72. On 2001, sequential was 71, simultaneous was 80, and composite was 73. These scores would be within the range of standard error of measurement and would indicate that KABC progress has been maintained.

Achievement scores administered in October 1998 and May 2001, indicate that on the TEMA standard score of 94 and 72, on the TEWL in 1998 was 81 and 2001 was 72, on the TERA in 1998 was 97 and 2001 was 61. All three of these scores indicate a decrease in performance..."

The school's test reasonably proved regression, but was it reasonable to blame the school for the regression? As the specialist and I talked, she really was very curious why we had stopped the intensive teaching once Sarah entered kindergarten. Intensive programming gave great gains, and once discontinued Sarah did not continue to make significant gains with what the district provided. I told the specialist I believed that the intense program had fulfilled its purpose of getting Sarah ready for integration into kindergarten. I mistakenly believed that she would continue to improve with the schools interventions. Even as I mulled all this over, I started to entertain the notion that Sarah had a unique learning curve, and that curve prohibited my expectations for her from coming to fruition. That and the preacher on the radio told me that the school's responsibility did not include being a god.

Sarah was such a unique challenge for everybody. One teacher graciously submitted answers to some questions I had about whether she felt prepared for the job of Sarah's teacher. The questions were part of my research during due process. They were probably the reason teachers went the other way when they saw me! The answers really pointed to the pressures that teachers were experiencing.

Ann Dunham

TEACHER'S THOUGHTS
I do not remember meeting with the autism team. I do remember meeting with the principal, a former teacher and a couple others. We met on the last day of school for teachers before summer vacation, for about (30 minutes). I was shown some of Sarah's work, her journal, drawings, and titles of books that she liked. EA was not there. In hindsight, I would have to say that I do not believe this was adequate preparation, but it was definitely more then I had ever been prepared for in the past concerning placement of children on IEPs in my classroom.

TRAINING & OTHER RESOURCES: I do feel that the EA was an excellent resource for Sarah and me but as far as tools for training, I did not receive such from the school administration. An example was when I requested film for an instamatic camera to make a picture schedule for Sarah and the wrong film was purchased. I was told that a camera for that film would be purchased but it never was. After a few weeks and a few reminders from me to a responsible party, I mentioned it to Ann and she offered a camera and film. But by then we were using a schedule with clock visual cues instead. If it were that difficult to get something so small, what would it take to get to go to a conference or go for training? Also, I have responsibilities to all children and is it right to take a school day or two to focus on meeting the needs of just one? Ann and EA were my main troubleshooters. I know that a specialist was at our school some of the time but she was very busy and I did not feel very approachable.

UNDERSTANDING HOW SARAH LEARNED: I feel that my understanding of Sarah's educative history was very clear because I had observed Sarah at her early childhood program and continued to follow her development in Kindergarten. Ann was very open about her expectations of and for Sarah and was more than willing to provide any information I requested. Under Siege by C. Park was very helpful to me. It helped me to understand that Sarah was going to make gains in different ways and stages than most children and backwards steps often accompanied that moving ahead. I also learned to celebrate everything and evaluate my own teaching as it related to all children in my room. Most important I learned that Sarah is more normal than she is different.

SPECIFIC TRAINING: I did not ask for specific training from the administration but I did request information from Barb and she came to our room twice to observe and help us problem solve on some issues. I do believe that Ann was the one to get those visits accomplished though. In hindsight, I realize that I should have gotten more educated and that there are many resources out there but the school day is limited and my family life is important too.

EVALUATIONS: ...I do not know of any true or objective way to test Sarah's ability at this time. But with every child, there is not one true way. Ongoing informal and formal observations as well as accumulative assessments are usually the most effective. It is also important to involve as many people as possible in the process of evaluating children who have major challenges because I, as the teacher, can only focus on so many things at once. I may miss something that others will pick up on.

UNDERSTANDING SARAH'S ABILITIES THROUGH TESTING: I believe that the information Ann provided for me helped me understand Sarah's abilities better than any of the information that was in her file. Ann's website is also an excellent resource that I have used. I cannot name any of the tests that she was administered, and I did not request any, but I am not acquainted with or trained to give many tests that the team uses. She did take a few accelerated reading tests in first grade but since we adapted them by reading the stories to her and then reading the questions, this was not a valid test. The tests that I am trained to give students measure their ability to read and write and these were not appropriate for Sarah in first grade. If there are tests out there to indicate her ability, I do not know what they are or what to even ask for.

FRUSTRATION IN TEACHING SARAH: I was confused on how to get Sarah to function at her full potential in a classroom of children who were moving ahead at a much faster pace. I was frustrated, but more with myself than with the district. I do not feel that I was trained and yet I am more trained than most teachers at this school. I took a year off to educate myself in meeting the needs of children with special needs and yet I know so little. Ann did not fail as an advocate for Sarah; in fact she is the best advocate I have ever met. She is also the best partner in the process of educating her daughter.

BUDGET CONCERNS: On the whole, it is obvious to me that budgetary needs are a definite drive in the decision making process before and after IEPs that I have been involved in. There are people on the team who advocate for meeting the needs of the children but hands and mouths are tied for various reasons. In Sarah's case I feel that it was more that people were led to believe that she functioned at a lower level than she was actually at, and so poor decisions were made during the process of placement and programs. A real concern that I had for her, and still have now, is that we lack a place for children with autism to go to when they are overcome with frustration. This would not only benefit them but others in the school who listen to them voice their frustrations through yelling and cries for help

That teacher's response helped me to understand the ambiguities behind completely knowing Sarah's capabilities. Any confusion about Sarah's capabilities seemed to necessarily default to the district's determinations during IEP. That fact only emphasized, to further degree, the need to find a team to help with next steps for teaching Sarah in our home. Maybe it would help to pre teach at home and then allow her to generalize by displaying what she had learned at school. Just like what happened with kindergarten. Our upcoming summer teaching team would come out of San Diego.

Chapter 8: Summer

Second In-home program, 2003 (ten years old). Right after school was out for Sarah's third grade year, a team from San Diego came to train our next in-home program group. Bobbie led that group. Barb worked alongside Bobbie and her team to provide input and cohesiveness, as far as information sharing on past programming and the development of the new program. Barb guided the new therapists through the summer while keeping in touch with the San Diego team. College students, a couple of high school students, and some of Sarah's former teachers came to our weekend workshop. My emphasis this time was simply to try to give Sarah tools for learning that showed what she knew across settings. In the past, as much as I tried to be Sarah's interpreter, the information I shared about her seemed to get lost in the shuffle, or in controversy. She needed the tools to independently show people her capabilities without my interpretations, and the in-home program provided such. One of Sarah's former teachers became very excited about our format and materials, because they addressed the needs for teaching in her resource room, expanding upon and complimenting what she already had in place in the classroom. Our in-home program seemed the best of both worlds because it was doable and complimentary to the public school, while also containing elements of the types of teaching that gave Sarah success in the past.

The successful elements of the summer program were as follows:
Token Economy
Nonverbal Actions—What do they mean?
Reciprocal Statements
What do you do or say when?

Outings and Pretend Play
Possessive Pronouns
Prepositions
Labeling by Feature
What do you see?
Noun Identification
Categories Intermixed
Math
Functional Money Identification
Addition and Subtraction
Word Problems
Applied Time
Measurement
Workbooks
Reading Word Families & Special Letter Clusters
Auditory Recall
Following Written Instruction
Sequencing Stories
Sequencing Pictures and Sentences
Independent reading time for reading book
Independent Tasks Workstation
Worksheets
Social Awareness

The summer was a time of purpose and structure for Sarah. My perception was that the therapists and former teachers who involved themselves in Sarah's program were having a great time seeing her experience success. Sarah is such a fascinating girl. While pleased about the learning materials that helped her in academics, I felt more excitement about the social aspects of the program. Those aspects brought forth an awareness of what a people person Sarah really is. She really likes having unique interactions with people. Barb reported some of those interactions in a programming report.

Examples of generalization of social awareness by Sarah
- *The first time we introduced the SD, "What do you say when someone says bye?" Sarah's response without prompt was, "Have a good day."*

Ann Dunham

- *During walks to the library, Sarah and Chelsea had been singing songs. On the way home from the library Sarah said to Chelsea, "You are my best friend," and gave her a hug.*
- *Jana was not feeling well and Sarah went up to her and asked, "Are you okay?"*
- *When Sarah's mom hit her head, Sarah said, "I'm sorry. Are you okay?"*
- *(9/30/03) Sarah was playing with a leaf she had taken off her plant and she wasn't paying attention, so I took it away. She was bothered and said, "Don't hurt the leaf!" I told Sarah to do a worksheet and she said, "I'm not." I told her she was and she said, "Oh, come on." (Ann)*
- *(10/30/03) On the way to Sinclair, Sarah pulled on my hand and said, "BJ, I want to go home." She then turned and pointed back the way we came and said, "Home is that way." (BJ)*
- *(11/4/03) Today Sarah was very chatty and energetic. She talked non-stop all the way to the library. It was hard to keep Sarah quiet in the library. The librarian even noticed and commented that it was the most she had ever heard Sarah talk.*
- *When returning from Post Net, Sarah walked past the dance studio. She stopped and looked at the class inside and then pointed to one of the girls and said, "A ballerina." She then copied what they were doing inside as she continued to walk home.*
- *As Sarah walked to the library she kept saying, "Its winter," because it was very chilly outside.*

At the time of this report, Sarah has been engaging in conversations with a variety of individuals, both in person and on the phone.

Sarah proved what she knew over the summer, with her strengths being easily evident. Sarah knew moods and emotions. She understood ways to respond in social situations, using those skills incidentally in natural settings. Outings were an absolute strength for her, and she generalized many skills during outings. She utilized many appropriate life skills to do with courtesy, such as waiting in line, taking turns, asking for help, and thanking people. Sarah engaged in simple conversations. She appropriately and successfully generalized math skills. Engaging in complex conversation remained an emerging skill for Sarah in drill situations, since following larger language load discussions required too much prompting. The processing of language was a great challenge for her. Conversation skills aside, she emerged wonderfully in her ability to express herself in writing. I had always seen her ability in this area because of her sequenced art, like the comic strips with which she would occupy her time. Her ability to express thoughts in writing, while always present, needed to be done in an acceptable way for the teachers. Some examples of sentences she generated on her own, after the summer teaching had been in force, follows.

Independent sentences, Summer 2003
- *Cheese is yummy.*
- *The grass is green.*
- *Kevin works at PostNet.*
- *The rain is wet.*
- *The dog is soft.*
- *I like to swim in the pool.*
- *Sonic is a hedgehog.*
- *Pringles are soaty (salty).*
- *Simba are road (roars).*
- *Yong (yawn) in is sleep.*
- *Tape is like glue.*
- *My garnen (garden) is growing.*
- *Box is emty (empty).*
- *Letter are something I write.*
- *The face is body.*
- *Street is a crossing.*
- *Is a farm is the sheep.*
- *The wheel is is bike.*
- *The paint is the red house.*
- *Teacher is in the class room.*
- *Scissors is cut.*

These sentences were generated entirely independently.
A journal entry that was independent: "Shining Star a toy. It is pink.

I want to buy one the Shining Star toy fun toy. McDonald's I ate french fries and chicken and soda."

Independent sentences from kindergarten for comparison.
* *Mom Dad Jeff Jana my fuem. (my family).*
* *I went wo trgert to baa mivea. (I went to Target to buy a movie).*
* *I lak two play out sas with looses. (I like to play outside with Lucy.)*
* *My two cookes tish the good.*
* *I rud my bak two be pok. (I rode my bike to the park.)*
* *We drove to to go boating in the lake.*
* *Mom and I wet rolandblade atder scoolo. (Mom and I went roller blading after school.)*
* *Dad bot me to schoolo today. Mom wet on a trip.*
These were independently written in Kindergarten. I would ask Sarah to tell me what they said and she would read them back to me.

From May to August, things went great. With the summer being such a success and the teaching materials from the in-home program being a good fit for Sarah, I decided to continue our program throughout her next school year. When the fourth grade year started, Sarah attended school for time in resource and specials since that time allowed her to generalize skills across settings, and to maintain already developed relationships with teachers and students. School started in August and then September came.

∽

SUMMER 2003
A complete review of the summer in-home program follows, and is derived from a written report to the San Diego team. This is a brief overview. For a comprehensive understanding of this programming, please contact Bobbie Kohrt. (bobbiekohrt@yahoo.com)

Token Economy
Sarah responded well to this. Reward system in which tokens are earned and then exchanged for back up reinforcers. This system evolved into a punch card system for some utilization at school.

Hello, Dr. Wells

Nonverbal Actions; What do they mean?
Mastered and generalized, and put on maintenance. Present a nonverbal gesture (yawning) and then ask, "What does this mean?" Ask her to "Show me (gesture)" Do not pair receptive and expressive trials. Practice incidentally/naturally as well as in a drill.

Reciprocal Statements
Mastered in drill situations. Therapist says "I have a _____." Sarah counters with "I have a_____." Another example, "My (object) is (color)." Also present a personal statement (from the list), as in "I am wearing_____," and then Sarah models similar statements about herself. Sarah needs to say the whole sentence. Two statements of personal information, "My birthday is _____" and "I am _____ years old."

What do you do/say when?
Mastered and generalized, and put on maintenance. "What do you say or do when_____?" Purpose is to increase ability to respond in social situations. Sarah used these incidentally in natural settings.

Asking & Formulating Questions
An emerging skill. Arrange familiar and unfamiliar items and prompt Sarah to ask "What is it?" or "What's that?" if she doesn't know what the object is. Present photos of known and unknown people and prompt Sarah to ask "Who is it?" if she doesn't know. Hide favorite objects and state tell Sarah "There is something hidden in the room." Prompt Sarah to ask "Where is it?" Extensions: "What are you doing?", "Where are you doing?", "Who has it?" and "What's wrong?"

Ask Me
Emerging. Statement, then question. Therapist says "I went to the store" and then Sarah responds with "What did you buy?" or "Where did you go?" To work on conversation skills Sarah should respond to a statement with a question about the statement.

Ann Dunham

Listening to Conversation

Not successful for Sarah in drill situations. However, we did know that she grabbed from bits of real life conversation as she would grab the car keys if we were talking about going somewhere. She would jump in the boat if we were talking about taking the boat out! The drill happened this way: Two people have a conversation that Sarah overhears. Therapist then asked where, when and who (in addition to what) questions. Do this drill at the beginning of the sessions.

Voice Volume

Have Sarah "Say (word) loud" or have her "Say (word) quietly." This is to increase voice volume during conversations.

Conversation

Read social story, review rules, and have Sarah pick a topic; three comments, three questions, rolling conversation with comments and questions.

Pretend Play and Outings

Engage in pretend play and go on outings in the community. The therapists only record when new skills or behaviors are observed. Nice weather permits the therapists to spend more time outside with Sarah for excursions, or going for a walk and engaging in conversations.

Excursions/social stories/independent task cards developed by Ann are as follows:
*   Eating out
*   Library
*   Church
*   Sinclair—generalized this to the math skill area, counting money by purchasing items available at Sinclair.
*   PostNet—developed an envelope template. Developed a notebook specific to PostNet outing that contains the letters that Sarah receives in response to the ones she sends, templates for the address and return address, templates for

the letters to be written. An additional function of this PostNet task is handwriting skills as Sarah uses lined paper with a red bottom line, and dotted center. It does compliment the writing a letter part of the Separate Life Skills notebook.

The trips have focused on Sinclair, PostNet, the library and sometimes McDonald's. In reviewing the notes, it appears that Sarah is becoming more verbal during these trips, and talking with individuals who work at these places. She is able to wait in line, take her turn, ask for assistance, and use routine phrases such as "thank you". She is talking more to the therapists and commenting more on her environment during these excursions. In addition, Ann had completed a digital storybook about Sarah's trip to the hairdresser. This story is used in a variety of drills. There were WH? prompts included in the book. This helped Sarah to generate sentences for the sequenced part of the drills.

Possessive Pronouns
This was mastered, generalized, and put on maintenance. "Touch __ ___'s nose", "Touch Sarah's shirt", "Whose (body part or clothing)?" Also used His/Her, Their/Our. In order to increase pronoun usage this was taught in written format during Independent Task Completion (ITC).

Prepositions
Inconsistently done by Sarah. Teach prepositions with the object as the agent, and Sarah as the agent. "Put the (object) (preposition) (location)", "Sit (preposition) (location)", "Where is it?" with the answer being one of the prepositions.

Labeling by feature
98 percent or above in mastery. "Which one has a (feature)?", "What (category) has a (feature)?" Written fill in the blank sentences, "A bird has _____," "An apple is a ____." To increase understanding of functions: "Find what you ____with", "What do you do with____?", "What would you use to ____?" and "You use

a (object) for _____"A word bank is provided. Will fade word bank to see if Sarah can be successful without it.

Expressive Actions

"What am I doing?" and "What is the boy/girl doing?" and "What did I do?" Intermix with present tense verbs. To increase understanding of irregular verbs and past tense.

Part Versus Whole

To increase object concepts. "What is this object?", "Name this part", "Fill in the correct label"

What do you see?

Mastered, generalized and put on maintenance. To increase expressive language and sentence structure. "What do you see?" (one object). "What do you see?" (two objects and conjunction). "Close your eyes, what's missing?"

Vocabulary Wall

Develop ability to identify and understand words/prewriting skill. Work with Sarah, putting words into appropriate categories on the vocabulary wall. Red poster for describing words (colors, feelings, shapes, textures, adverbs, smell, taste, etc). Blue poster for nouns. Extensive vocabulary wall. We need to determine if Sarah is effectively utilizing this word wall. Is she able to transfer this information to worksheets that she is doing?

Noun Identification

Increase language art skills. Identification of nouns in a written sentence by cue "Circle the nouns in the sentence". Place new nouns on the word wall.

Multiple Component Naming

Increase the ability to label an item with attributes. Building up to three components where the cue is "What do you see?" and the response must have three differing attributes. Sarah experienced difficulty with this. She would perseverate with a single component when doing drill (such as color). Therapists are prompting to elicit other attributes. With prompts, Sarah is producing attributes other then color but the order of presentation does not follow normal word order (i.e., size, texture, shape, and color).

Categories Intermixed
Some sessions, 100 percent level one rating…so sometimes it seemed mastered, but mastery was not consistent. Increase expressive language. "Name a _____ (food)," "A_____ (bird) is _____ (animal)," and "A _____ (hammer or dog) is a_____ (tool or animal)."

Vocabulary Concepts
Increase synonym, antonyms, definitions. "What is the definition of_____?", "Tell me another word for_____" and "Tell me a word that means opposite of _____".

Absurdities
Increase ability to develop awareness of the environment. "Tell me what is wrong with this picture."

Language concepts: Labels, functions, and categories
Mastered in drill situations. Increase the ability to understand language concepts. "What is this?" (Banana), "What is a banana?" (Food), "What do you do with a banana? (You eat it).

Opposites
Increase expressive language and flexibility. Use pictures. "Find the opposite of _____" and "What is the opposite of _____?"

Math: Money Identification
Mastered, generalized and moved to maintenance. Community skills and mathematics. "Find the (money)" and "What is it?"

Functional Money Identification
Workbook, worksheets mastered 98 percent of the time, and emerging in real life. Increase community skills and mathematics. Pennies only, counting up to twenty-five cents. Nickels only, counting up to fifty cents. Dimes only, counting up to fifty cents. Pennies and nickels, counting up to twenty-five cents. Pennies and dimes,

counting to fifty cents. Shop for items…label toys/snacks/etc with price tag, and have Sarah shop for the items. Independent workbook practice. Sarah counted money to buy items at Sinclair and PostNet.

Addition and Subtraction

Mastery at 90 percent. The teacher was excited to observe that Sarah was doing double digit with regrouping subtraction with no visual prompts, "Wow. Did independently. Did not use pic symbols." Increase addition and subtraction skills. Write a few problems on a sheet of paper, 0 – 10. Remember to use the touch math principles. Teach regroup via the lesson prior to putting it in an independent task. Incorporate both addition and subtraction problems on the same page. Continue to practice single digit problems.

Word Problems

Increase addition and subtraction skills. "Read and do problem." Independent workbooks and worksheets, ITC. Use addition and subtraction word list provided. Mastery 90 percent of the time. It is felt that a higher language level will cause difficulty for Sarah. Example: If there are 4 ice cream cones and 5 children are there enough for everyone?

Telling Time

Sarah does well on the applied time drills and her response is in digital time. Increase beginning telling time skills (analog clock). "Find_____o'clock" and "What time is it?" Do not pair expressive with receptive. Independent workbook practice. Begin to use different language (half past, quarter past, quarter after, quarter til, ten til, twenty til, ten after, twenty after). Listed as time intermixed trials on data sheet. Expansion has not been addressed. Difficulty in all but the half past. Question was raised asking the importance of using different language.

Applied Time

Sarah had mastered this skill. Community skills and application of time skills. During the sessions, periodically ask "What time is it now?"

Hello, Dr. Wells

Greater and Less than Discrimination

Sarah got it right about 50 percent of the time. Increase math skills. Sarah needs to indicate understanding of greater than and less than. Tried pairing the symbols with the word prompts of: more, less, bigger, smaller. Sarah's ability increased with the word prompts.

Measurement

Done correctly 95 percent of the time. Increase grade appropriate math skills. "Measure this object." Inches, feet and centimeters.

Addition and Subtraction

Continue to add to the addition/subtraction drill making it more difficult and moving from double to triple digit.

Workbooks

Purchase more money/time/word problem workbooks moving through first grade and on.

Reading: Letter Sounds

Mastery 95 percent of the time. Consonants and word families. Set A: unk, ot, ar, ub, or, en, ing, og, ow, ash, an, aw. Set B: ate, ack, ait, ad, old, ank, ap, ug, all, ain, ight, ell, ound. Set C: ide, in, ore, ink, ick, ur, er, ale, id, ame, ar, ir, ice. Special letter cluster: tion, ght, ealth, ough, ing, view, ease, ior, ium, ory.

Phonetic Awareness

She mastered it on some days, and then other days the rating is at 2 or 3. Increase phonetic awareness with word decoding. Increase awareness while reading. Have Sarah "sound out the word".

Answering WH Questions: With Photos

Increase understanding of wh-questions. "Who is it?", "What is he/she doing?" and "Where is he/she?"

Sorting by WH Questions

Increase understanding of wh-questions. Sort photos of people, places, and things into "who," "where," and "what" piles. "This is a person. Person, we ask 'who' question. Put with the persons". Same with "place" and "thing".

Super Duper Wh-Questions Books
Required prompting. Increase understanding of wh-questions. Tell a short story about the picture then review the questions. Complete the booklet until mastered. Continue to practice the story without the booklet. Target books: Restaurant and Post Office.

Auditory Recall
Increase memory tasks. Repeating a series of: two word, three word, two numbers, three numbers. Ask Sarah "What did I say?" Mastery ninety-eight percent of the time.

Following written instructions: Word Hunt
Increase functional use of reading, "Read this and do what it says." This will increase attention to follow and finish tasks independently. Independent Task Completion (ITC). Ninety percent mastery.

Sequencing Familiar
Increase the ability to sequence and story tell. "Put the cards in order." and "Tell me a story about the cards." Increase to 4/5 cards. Prompt/assist Sarah to tell complete sentences for the story. Limited data available but this drill was engaged in frequently by the girls. The 1–3 rating system without ability to comment was reason for lack of data. Picture sequencing is mastered. Story telling requires prompts. Sarah did begin to generate sentences independently in a coherent sequence when the stories were familiar or involved an activity she was actually involved in.

Sequencing Pictures and Sentences: Independent Task Completion (ITC)
Increase the ability to sequence a story. "Put the pictures and sentences in order." Sarah then cuts and puts the sentences and pictures in order. Mastery ninety-five percent of the time.

Hello, Dr. Wells

Sequencing Sentences
Increase the ability to sequence and story tell. Therapist writes three sentences. Has Sarah "Put the sentences in order." and then "Read the story to me in order." Mastery ninety-five percent of the time.

Independent Reading Time
Increase the amount of independent time. "Time for free reading." and Sarah reads for 5 minutes. Therapists ask specific WH questions about the story. Sarah reads for the set amount of time. Wh questions are emerging.

Reading Comprehension
Increase attention to stories and conversations. Therapist tells a short story with specific details. Then tells Sarah to "Find the right picture." Then asks specific questions about the short story.

Reading Comprehension: Worksheets
Increase attention to stories and comprehension. Sarah reads to decode. Sarah reads again for fluency. Sarah finishes the comprehension questions independently. Review and correct. Sarah has learned that on the worksheets the answers to the comprehension questions are in the same order as the questions are listed. It is Ann's impression that Sarah is merely writing the responses in rote order as they are on the sheet.

Workbooks
Continue to extend the reading comprehension.

Inferences
Oral Directions
Increase attention to follow oral instructions. Read statement and have Sarah complete item. When completed review and correct the page by reading the statements again and telling Sarah if she completed the item correctly.

Alphabetic Ordering
Increase spelling and pre-dictionary skills. Spelling lists. Begin with three words and have her put them in order, "Put these words in ABC order."

Ann Dunham

Writing: I Spy

Objects are placed on a table, the therapist describes the object, and Sarah guesses. Or objects are placed on the table and Sarah describes them with the therapist guessing. Some days are mastery at one-hundred percent. Others are fifty percent. Cortney introduced a visual prompt. When she did this with the first presentation Sarah understood what was expected and did the subsequent presentation accurately without the prompt. Prompt looks like this: "I spy something that is_____. It is_____. It is _____. What is it?" The prompt was faded. Sometimes Sarah will say "I spy something that is a ball, it is red and white" or "I spy something that is a dog, it is soft and brown." So she is giving her I spy away!

Sentence Writing

Sarah is generating short simple sentences, but often requires assistance in using correct word order. Examples (as written by Sarah):

- *Cheese is yummy.*
- *The grass is green.*
- *Kevin works at PostNet.*
- *The rain is wet.*
- *The dog is soft.*
- *I like to swim in the pool.*
- *Sonic is a hedgehog.*
- *Pringles are soaty (salty).*
- *Simba are road (roars).*
- *Yong in is sleep. (I yawn when I am sleepy.)*
- *Tape is like glue.*
- *My garnen (garden) is growing.*
- *Box is emty.*
- *Letter are something I write.*
- *The face is body.*
- *Street is a crossing.*
- *Is a farm is the sheep.*
- *The wheel is is bike.*
- *The paint is the red house.*
- *Teacher is in the class room.*
- *Scissors is cut.*

The therapist corrected the sentence and then Sarah wrote it correctly.

Sentence Writing
Increase ability to understand a chosen word and use it appropriately. "Write a sentence with the word _____ in it."

Journal Writing
Increase ability to describe daily events. Sarah writes name and date on paper. Sarah writes sentences about an event. She draws a picture of the event. She does well on generating topics but continues to need significant assistance in writing full sentences. One good sample of an entry done independently by Sarah: "Shining Star a toy. It is pink. I want to buy one the Shining Star toy fun toy. McDonald's I ate french fries and chicken and soda."

Topic Board
Increase expressive language skills. Sarah labels the following items about an object: name, shape, function, color, size. Therapist wrote the words and then prompt/shape the sentences. Sarah was writing sentences for each of the topic board cues. We watched for noun/verb agreement in sentences.

Life Skills: Phone call practice

Life Skills: Vocabulary Theme
Requested that the theme be related to SD content standards for Sarah's appropriate grade level. Additional materials were received from Tricia. Vocabulary Identification, Art, Picture to word matching, Language, Cooking, Games, Science.

Fun Popcorn Science Project
A file folder that Ann developed for Sarah had instructions for the project posted on the inside left hand side of the folder. Observation chart was taped to the right hand side of the folder. The project itself was in a colored envelope. The summary of the project was on the outside of the envelope. Individual steps were on the inside

cover of the envelope and the materials needed were in the envelope.

Typing
Ann attempted to use a keyboarding program from Jump Start. It was not effective with Sarah. She is now checking into Type to Learn Junior which is the program being used by the school district.

Cooking
Use cooking activities with Boardmaker directions. Ann developed a "Cooking and Especially Baking" notebook. Goes with the Separate Life Skills notebook. Each individual recipe includes the recipe from the book with a picture and instruction sheet. Instructions are also written on spiral bound 3" x 5" index cards with one instruction per card.

Example:
- *Heat oven to 350°.*
- *Spray pan with cooking spray.*
- *Spoon peanut butter cookie dough in pan.*
- *Press dough with floured fingers to make crust.*
- *Put in oven for 16 to 19 minutes.*
- *Take out of oven and sprinkle marshmallows on crust.*
- *Put in oven for 2 or 3 minutes.*
- *Take out of oven and sprinkle with M&Ms.*
- *Melt chocolate chips and oil with low heat.*
- *Drizzle over treat.*
- *Let cool for 45 min.*
- *Eat!*

Activity summary cards on 5" x 8" index cards with digital pictures. Each card contained a short summary of what was done. Card 1: Marshmallows, M&M's and peanut butter crust were the ingredients to my treat (three pictures of the ingredients). Card 2: We spread the marshmallows on our peanut butter crust. Then we put it in the oven to melt the marshmallows (two pictures of activity). Card 3: I melted the chocolate to drizzle on our treat.

We already sprinkled M&M's on the melted marshmallows (one picture). Card 4: We all had fun drizzling the chocolate on our treats! (two pictures).

Writing a Letter: Ann developed a notebook specific to this outing. It contains letters that Sarah receives in response to the ones she sends, templates for the addresses, and return addresses and templates for the letters to be written.

Workbooks
Books utilized for Sarah's programming:
- Grammar Skills, first grade level, Rainbow Bridge Publishing
- Language Arts Core Skills, Grade 1, Steck – Vaughn
- Parts of Speech Nouns, Verbs and Adjectives, Grades 2 & 3, Teacher Created Materials
- Language Arts, Grade 2, School Zone
- Super Duper Questions booklets, Elementary, Super Duper Publications
- Clues to Comprehension, 1 & 2, Evan – Moor
- Comprehension Curriculum of Basic Skills, Level 2, McGraw – Hill
- Just a Minute Math, Elementary, Steck – Vaughn
- Daily Word Problems, Grade 1, Evan – Moor
- Math Central, K, Houghton

Independent Tasks / Workstation
This is a workstation where Sarah works independently. There is no conversation. If Sarah exhibits inappropriate behavior, she is presented with "check your behavior" cards and this will generally cause the behavior to stop.

Worksheets
Used Independent Task Completion focused on the following. Nouns, adjectives, pronouns, following directions, listening, sequencing, addition, subtraction, ordinal numbers, riddles, reading comprehension, WH questions, and measuring.

Ann Dunham

Worksheets for School

Focused on time, reading comprehension, pronouns, money counting, and dictionary skills. Ann developed a system where the worksheets are placed in a pocket folder. Each sheet has a sticker in the lower right hand corner. As each sheet is completed, Sarah puts the sticker on a square on the inside of the pocket folder (up to eight squares per folder). Sarah places the finished work sheet in the right pocket of the folder.

Chapter 9: September Comes

Psychosis ensues, 2003 (ten years old). A planning meeting occurred at school before Sarah's fourth grade year. The previous year's due process with the district probably added a dash of tension to the mix of any meeting. Now I focused on my personal responsibility to provide opportunities in learning for Sarah, and it seemed like we had a good plan in place for helping her to realize forward progress. During the meeting, I enthusiastically shared about our in-home program and the excitement I felt about its continuation. For the most part, my hope continued to be that Sarah might gain ability in generalizing her skills across settings, and across slightly different types of materials. It seemed like a more doable hope since Sarah's placement in resource provided materials and teaching more specific to her learning challenges. The first days of fourth grade came without a hitch. It felt so great. An email from one teacher said it all.

> ...The changes in Sarah are phenomenal. She is seemingly happy all the time. She makes eye contact. She is speaking in sentences. She came up to me yesterday and said, "I need to go to the bathroom." Today we met another teacher outside the bathroom and the teacher said hi to Sarah. Without any prompting from me Sarah looked at the teacher and said, "Hi Mrs. B." I am just so thrilled with this part of Sarah's maturity, progress. Call it what you will. She shared cookies again today—asked each person. She has two left—enough for snack tomorrow. She is a bright light in my day. Chris (teacher)

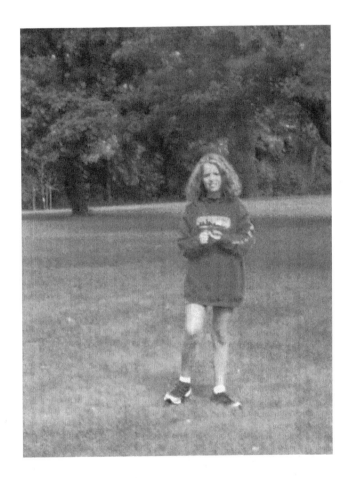

Sarah 2003

Ann Dunham

When September came, after the first few weeks of school, Sarah began to exhibit verbally aggressive behavior. I did not know what to attribute the worsening behavior to, since she had not been verbally or physically aggressive towards others. One teacher told me that Sarah reached out and grabbed her throat while they did worksheets together, for no observable reason. Sarah complied when asked to let go, but it was out of character and so the teacher felt great concern. As I heard about behaviors cropping up at school, I also became concerned about things that started to happen at home. Sarah started to walk in circles, sideways or backwards while seeming confused. One afternoon she called for me, and upon checking on her, I found that she forgot to pull her pants down before using the bathroom. From then on, she seemed confused about the process of going to the bathroom. I also started to notice occasions when Sarah squished herself between the bed and the wall, or she hid in her walk-in closet; that is how I found her when I woke her up in the morning. None of these things ever happened before.

Towards Thanksgiving break, Sarah manifested willful aggression towards staff at school, with indications of hitting, spitting, biting, and blowing indicated in a school-written social story for teaching expectations. These behaviors happened at school, but not at home, so I did not have an immediate awareness about the ongoing nature of them. Perhaps the school felt it was a natural progression of her autism, but the sticking point for me continued to be the fact that she never showed violence towards others in the entirety of her school history. Unfortunately, the aggressive negative behaviors started to happen at home. Upon hearing that teachers needed to use force to carry Sarah out of a class, I decided to take her out of school, since that is where the negative patterns first manifested. I wanted to see them stop. Taking her out of school was not too problematic since we had the in-home program. Things went okay for a very short while at home, but eventually she hit me; on another occasion, she pointed scissors and then a pen at me in an aggressive manner. She also started displaying these types of things towards the in-home therapists. Within the same period, there came a night when I heard Sarah scream, and upon investigating, I found that she sliced her throat with scissors. The next day, Barb asked her why she did it. Her response, "Scissors are a sword." In a weird combination of hindsight and being blindsided, immediately after the scissor incident, I found that Sarah had been watching cartoons with some very aggressive themes. She watched them during her down time while upstairs, and I figured that out because of the need to watch her more closely after the scissor incident. I did not know that such garbage would be available alongside the more benign cartoons. The anime of Inuyasha and others would do battle with Sarah from this time on, and I hated them for it. The angry, aggressive, and supernatural themes affected Sarah and because of them, it seemed she could not handle being alone. Exposure to the anime commercials even pushed her off a behavioral cliff. Even as the anime was bad for her, it beckoned her; I felt like I was watching her deal with a drug habit when I observed her dual nature as she wanted to watch it, and did not want to watch it all at the same time. It seemed like someone dealing with chemical dependency.

Ann Dunham

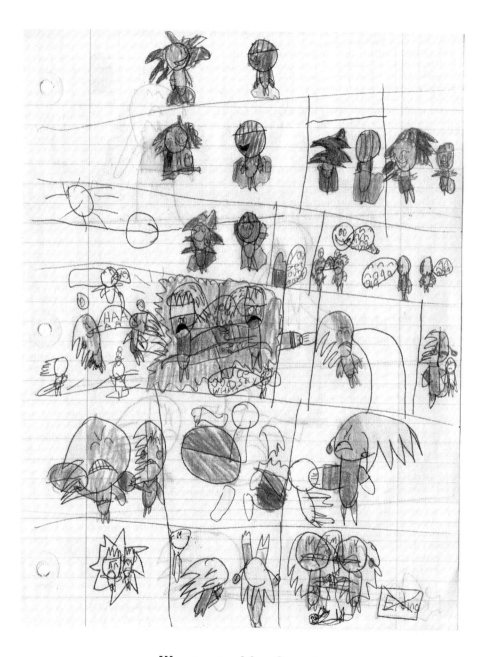

Illustrated by Sarah

Hello, Dr. Wells

Not very long into the days of her worsening, Sarah started to touch her groin area and poke around her eyes in a one-two type succession, and she seemed spacey while doing such. We attempted to stop her, but she became angry about our intercessions. I feared that her behavior might result in an eye infection or damage, so I took her to three different doctors. The results of the visits: it is a stimulatory behavior, her eyes are irritated so wash around them, and maybe it is a sinus infection. They were just trying, as was I. As hard as everyone tried, the day came when Sarah beat me up. On that day before Thanksgiving, we visited the emergency room, but not for me. I felt sure that a tumor caused the drastic change in my daughter, because she was off the charts different. I did not accept the worsening as part of her autism. I did not accept the explanation about puberty being the culprit. I had a hard time with finding everything to blame, when relief continued to be out of sight. I wanted to keep looking for a cause that had a cure, so that she might have relief.

From then on things became quite rough. Sarah physically aggressed towards me at times, and not always for any particular reason; meaning sometimes it happened when I did not let her have something, but mostly it happened when I tried to keep her from hurting herself when she engaged in one of those nonsensical rages. At Christmas time, we noticed that she did weird things with her eyes, and she coupled that with head movements. She made a weird type of utterance with the head movement. At times, she gazed in a crazed way, and then moved from a harmless activity in a different room in order to find someone to push or grab, that person having nothing to do with any sort of negative event. Could it get any worse? Sarah improved in her conversation abilities, but those talks happened with non-existent persons. I did not appreciate the language improvement, because I had preoccupation with the daily aggression. She started to beat me daily and sometimes multiple times daily, usually doing so because I tried to stop her from self-injury, when she listened to Getty, the voice in her head.

New Years Eve found us at the psychiatrist's office. He listened intently as we described the events leading to the emergency visit with him.

After listening, he told us he understood the situation, having seen it experienced by other familys. Because of his experience, he felt that Sarah would probably not get better, no matter what we tried. He added that she might even get worse. He asked us to consider placing her somewhere. We told him that we understood why he felt that way, but our inclination remained that of helping Sarah at home, not institutionalizing her. He agreed to help us in our endeavors to find a medication that would help, and as he helped by beginning medication trials, I wrote some explanations of her episodes. She tried Risperdal (r), Seroquel (s), and then Zoloft (z).

Three Weeks of Med Trials
- *(1/7/04) Sarah and I are in the car. Sarah is in the back seat. I hear her say, "Get a needle Sarah. I am going to poke your eyes out." r*
- *(1/8/04) We are getting in the car. Sarah screams a high-pitched blood curdling scream. She says, "We have to stop him. Getty is upstairs. Help Mommy!" r*
- *(1/8/04) Sarah says, "Come on Sarah. Go upstairs," but she does not want to go upstairs as she is in the kitchen eating breakfast. She tells herself, "No!" I tell Sarah she can eat her breakfast and everything is okay...she does not have to go upstairs. r*
- *(1/9/04) She wanted fries but could not eat them on her own. Even though she asked for them and I gave them to her, she walked away. She asks for the fries again. I give them to her. She walks away again. She goes up to her room. She looks toward the ceiling and tells me that the house is gone, gesturing toward the ceiling. Before this, her jaw was tight. r*
- *(1/18/04) We are driving on the freeway. Sarah is in front. We have her favorite food. Sarah cannot eat it. Her arms are up behind her head because she put them that way. Sarah asks me to help. I put chicken in her mouth. She chews, swallows some, and spits some out. This goes on for a while. Sarah actually grabs her drink. Then she yells and throws it upside down. She gets the bag of food. She has told me that she wants to eat it. But she folds the bag shut while yelling at Getty. She*

is screaming and yelling as she throws the bag of food on the floor. She stomps the bag several times while continuing to scream. Now she cries. She kicks the dashboard and windshield. She starts turning so she can kick in my direction. I am holding one of her hands while I drive because she starts to squirm out of her seat belt. She tries to bite my hand, but then backs away. She bangs on the passenger side window. She is talking to Getty. She asks me to get new food. I cannot because I fear the same thing will happen again. s

- (1/19/04) Sarah is taking a bath. She has always loved the bath. Getty shows up. Sarah starts throwing her face into the bath water. She comes up when she is out of air. She becomes frantic and screams for help. While this is occurring, as is the case in every instance, I try to explain that Getty is not real and she does not have to listen. Sometimes she can handle it better than others. This particular time Jeff had to help me get her out of the tub before she hurt herself. s

- (1/21/04) Sarah is happy and enjoying a movie with her father. As if someone flipped a switch, she starts to scream and argue with Getty. She is striking out at things that are not there. She looks right through her father as her tries to calm and console her. This goes on for approximately 10 minutes. Just an hour before all of this Sarah was uncontrollably laughing without being able to stop. That went on for a half hour. z

- (1/23/04) Sarah is with Wayne and me at Perkins. We are at the table and everything is fine. At first, Sarah is quite calm. She becomes quite animated and talkative. She asks to use the bathroom. We do so. We return to the table. Our food arrives. We begin to eat. Sarah wants to eat but cannot seem to do it and asks for help. I assist Sarah with eating and as she chews, her eyes get this weird gaze. It seems like the weird gaze is associated with chewing or swallowing. She eats some and spits very little out. This goes on for a short time. All of a sudden, she slumps in her seat. She then lies along the whole seat (bench style) face down. She begins to scream and cry for help. I try to calm her, to help her sit up. I try to assure her and tell her everything is okay. She is not mad at me; she is just not *consolable. She lays there as if she cannot move. My brother picks her up and helps her to stand. She screams and cries as we leave. I try to calm her with the fact that we can take the food with us. She cries as we are in the car. I reassure her some more. She calms down. My brother gets to the car with the food. I feed her in the car. She seems happier now. We drive and the entire route home she has her mouth wide open against the back of my seat. She asks for help and I am able to sit her up straight against her own back seat. But she returns to the position of having her mouth on the back seat. z*

The medications proved to be ineffective. The psychiatrist and I engaged in a difficult exchange. During an office visit, I lamented about how everyone just wants to medicate without finding the etiology behind the problem. I felt frustrated. He felt frustration as well; because he answered my comment by mentioning how easy his job might be if my reporting about Sarah's behaviors and function, past and present, were not so inconsistent. I took that as a form of correction. I went home and reviewed every report on Sarah, and then I made an excel spreadsheet of her behaviors through the following age periods: three to six, six and seven, seven to ten, and ten and eleven.

Observation (not at all, seldom, occasionally, frequently, ongoing)	Preschool 3–6	Kindergarten 6–7	Elementary 7–10	Since Sept 3 10	Noted before or after January trials (before, after, or comment)
Forgetting to pull pants down while using toilet	Not yet potty trained	Not at all	Not at all	Seldom	Before
Confusion in ability to use bathroom	Not yet potty trained	Not at all	Not at all	Ongoing	Before
Forgetting how to use bathroom	Not at all	Not at all	Not at all	Occasionally	After/Stands up while she is trying to go
General confusion with operating Computer, TV, VCR, DVD & remotes	Not at all	Not at all	Not at all	Ongoing	Before
Asking for help to move from one room to another	Not at all	Not at all	Not at all	Frequently to ongoing	After
Confusion when eating, swallowing and spitting food out	Not at all	Not at all	Not at all	Frequently	After
Confusion in moving from laying to sitting, sitting to standing, rolling side to side	Not at all	Not at all	Not at all	Frequently to ongoing	Before
Jaw locking	Not at all	Not at all	Not at all	Frequently	After
Spacey	Not at all	Not at all	Seldom	Frequently	
Drooling	Not at all	Not at all	Not at all	Occasionally to frequently	After
Tongue	Not at all	Not at all	Not at all	Occasionally to frequently	After
Involuntary tongue movement	Not at all	Not at all	Not at all	Not at all	After
Weird eye gaze while chewing	Not at all	Not at all	Occasionally	Ongoing	Before
Weird or crazed eye gaze	Not at all	Not at all	Seldom	Ongoing	Before
Walking in circles or backward with blank look on face	Not at all	Not at all	Not at all	Ongoing	Before
Moving head from side to side while making utterances	Not at all	Not at all	Not at all	Frequently	Before
High pitch scream, no observable cause	Not at all	Not at all	Not at all	Frequently	Before
High pitch scream, throw object, no cause	Not at all	Not at all	Not at all	Frequently	Before
Loss of awareness	Not at all	Not at all	Seldom	Frequently	Before

Ann Dunham

Holding up arms as if a prisoner for no observable reason	Not at all	Not at all	Not at all	Frequently	After
Involuntary leg movements	Not at all	Not at all	Not at all	Frequently	After
Inability to take step or stand upright	Not at all	Not at all	Not at all	Frequently	After
Spasms in lower body	Not at all	Not at all	Not at all	Occasionally	Before
Giggling for no reason	Occasionally	Occasionally	Occasionally	Occasionally	Before
Self talk (cartoon talk)	Occasionally	Occasionally	Frequently	Seldom	Before
Talking and arguing with her internal conflict	Not at all	Not at all	Not at all	Ongoing	Before
Set phrases followed by violence, anger, sadness and conflict	Not at all	Not at all	Not at all	Ongoing	Before
Rolling eyes upward or around	Not at all	Not at all	Seldom	Frequently	Before
Applying pressure to and around the eyes with hands or fingers	Not at all	Not at all	Not at all	Frequently	Before
Touching groin then eyes in succession	Not at all	Not at all	Not at all	Frequently	Before
Tears as if crying but not crying	Not at all	Not at all	Not at all	Occasionally	Before
Grabbing a person throat for no reason	Not at all	Not at all	Not at all	Frequently	Before
Coming from other room or enjoyable activity in order to forcefully push/ grab another	Not at all	Not at all	Not at all	Frequently	Before
Stabbing people with pencils	Not at all	Not at all	Not at all	Occasionally	Before
Hitting others	Not at all	Not at all	Not at all	Frequently to ongoing	Before
Spitting at others	Not at all	Not at all	One time	Occasionally	Before
Self injury	Not at all	Not at all	See note	Occasionally	Before
Cutting throat	Not at all	Not at all	Not at all	One time	Before
Throwing self down stairs	Not at all	Not at all	Not at all	One time	Before
Frequent trips to bathroom, even waking to do so (IC)	Not at all	Not at all	Frequent to not at all	Not at all	Before / Interstitial Cystitis
Drinking way too much	Not at all	Not at all	Seldom	Not at all	Before / Interstitial Cystitis

Hello, Dr. Wells

Telling me "throat frozen"	Not at all	Not at all	Not at all	Frequently	Before
Telling me "poops are frozen"	Not at all	Not at all	Occasionally	Frequently	Before
Bad breath	Not at all	Not at all	Seldom	Occasionally	Before
Body odor	Not at all	Not at all	Not at all	Frequently	After
Squeezing legs together as stim	Not at all to seldom	Seldom	Frequently	Seldom to not at all	Before
Sitting as uncomfortable	Not at all	Not at all	Ongoing	Occasionally	Before
Touching objects to face	Frequently	Seldom	Not at all	Not at all	Stopped
Mouthing objects	Ongoing	Occasionally	Seldom	Ongoing	Stopped
Sticking fingers in her mouth	Seldom	Not at all	Not at all	Ongoing	After
Index finger on front teeth as if measuring	Not at all	Not at all	Not at all	Ongoing	After
Eating hair	Frequently	Seldom	Not at all	Seldom	Before / Stopped
Eating Barbie hands and feet	Not at all	Not at all	Not at all	Ongoing	Before / Stopped
Eating blanket fringe	Not at all	Not at all	Occasionally	Not at all	Before
Eating shirt collar	Not at all	Not at al	Not at all	Ongoing	Before
Drinking Lysol	One time	Not at all	Not at all	Not at all	Before
Ate nut (i.e. nut & bolt)	Not at all	Not at all	One time	Not at all	Before
Getting in full tub with clothes on	Not at all	Not at all	Not at all	Frequently	Before
Drawing on carpet with markers	Not at all	Not at all	Not at all	Occasionally	Before
Getting into lotions and toiletries	Not at all	Not at all	Seldom	Occasionally	Before
Using lotion for art on carpet	Not at all	Not at all	Not at all	Occasionally	Before
Public Address sensitivity, treble sounds	Ongoing	Ongoing	Ongoing	Ongoing	Before
Body heating up from exposure to PA system	Not at all	Not at all	Occasionally	Occasionally	Before
Light sensitivity (eyes)	Not at all	Occasionally	Occasionally	Occasionally	Before
Playing videogames	Not at all	Frequently	Frequently	Frequently to not at all	Used to like but stopped
Art and drawing	Occasionally	Frequently to ongoing	Frequently	Seldom to not at all	Used to like but stopped
Independent navigation on computer to: print pages while making her own stories, find sites of interest, play games and find pictures	Not at all	Seldom	Ongoing	Ongoing to not at all	Used to like but stopped

Fortunately, Sarah's developmental doctor provided documentation of yearly observations and concerns. I did find things in the reports that I forgot. She ate non-food items from time to time throughout her history. She engaged in various benign oddities from time to time. Most important to the psychiatrist was the fact that she tried Paxil for suspected obsessive-compulsive tendencies in the spring of 2003. However, her problem ended up being interstitial cystitis. The Paxil made her violent when titrated up to full dose and it did not help with the frequent trips to the bathroom. What helped was identifying that she had interstitial cystitis and then treating her for it. Detrol stopped the frequent trips to the bathroom. The forgotten things represented blips on the radar of a very large field of things that I needed to remember. The doctor report alluding to successful treatment with Paxil added insult, since it did not have benefit of providing more important updated information. Even with all the consideration about what I missed telling the doctor, there was also the fact that my view of Sarah, was that of a severely autistic child doing much better than expected up to the recent worsening; and so that is how I described her to the doctor at the initial visit. I did not intend to mislead, but that description did noting for the doctor, who needed to have some specific data to pull from in order to know Sarah's unique baseline. All disagreements aside, the local psychiatrist agreed to refer Sarah to Mayo.

Chapter 10: Broken

Schizophrenia, 2004 (eleven years old). As we prepared for the Mayo trip, I wrote a couple of my own reports on Sarah for the doctors. Communicating in writing worked better, as it seemed more efficient and complete. Sarah would get to know many doctors at Mayo. They would read my written explanations, but also compare them with years of differing doctors' reports.

At Mayo, a neurologist examined Sarah and reviewed her history. She called the problems episodic with some automatisms. She ordered an EEG. If the EEG indicated nothing, then there would be a referral to psychiatry for another try at medicating. The first EEG did not indicate seizure. We spent some days at a hotel while we waited for a visit with the psychiatrist. It was difficult to have Sarah in a hotel with her troubles being what they were. One time, while she tried to enjoy a movie her head moved from side to side and her legs jerked, as if involuntary. That activity repeated itself. Another time, she was sitting there and her tongue was just all over the place; she was drooling and she was spacey. She then found time to argue with Getty, and while doing so, she lost her balance and almost passed out. She picked up imaginary things and then trapped them, similar to some recent episodes at home. We tried taking her out to Perkins in Rochester, in order to change things up, but she repeated the events from a recent January episode at our local Perkins. That is to say, eating there became a trigger, or the reason for the episode. Along with everything else, the inexplicable screaming due to what she heard in her head remained ongoing. Finally, the visit to the psychiatrist happened.

The doctor met us in the lobby and invited us back to her office. She looked through some things about Sarah's history and then started to talk with us. As we were talking, out of the blue Sarah started hallucinating. The doctor rolled back in her chair so she could get full view of what was going on. She got a very serious look on her face and yet at the same time was absolutely shocked. She stated very emphatically that Sarah was hallucinating. We looked at her and nodded in agreement. We told her that it felt as if nobody believed us. The doctor sent us home with as needed Thorazine to give to Sarah when we felt an episode might be coming on. We headed home and would come back on the day of the scheduled video EEG.

(1/30/04) We are on our way back from Rochester. Sarah wakes up from a nap in the car. She had previously had one of her episodes in the psychiatrist office at Mayo. She has had a rough time throughout the morning, one of the rougher ones. After she wakes up, she begins to become agitated. She is arguing with Getty and Mr. Winky. We cannot talk her through it. She begins to slam the car window and kick the back of the driver's seat. I attempt to hold her hands so that she does not hurt herself while slamming and punching things in the car. She begins to try to hit and bite me. She gets my hair and does not let go. I tell Steve to pull over so I can drive. She is too quick and strong for me. Steve is in the back seat with Sarah. He too, has a difficult time restraining Sarah from hurting herself while she is out of control in the back seat. It goes on for quite some time and then the one-time use medication that the psychiatrist gave us kicks in. Sarah calms, and she cries. While crying she says she is sorry. Thorazine 10 mg

(1/31/04) Sarah asks me and Jana, "What is wrong with Sarah?" I tell her not to worry and that we will find out and she will be okay. In the evening Sarah says, "Momma, I love you," and kisses and hugs me. Used Thorazine when she was getting revved up.

Sarah was simply using as-needed Thorazine. We returned to Mayo several days later for another try at finding the underlying cause of things. Truth be known, I would be hitting my absolute bottom in the days that followed. The video EEG was successful in that they were able to record many of Sarah's episodes. They did rule out actual seizures. Most of the episodes they recorded involved the weird eye gaze, with verbal utterances and head movements. The report alluded to diagnoses of Autism spectrum, Schizoid features, multiple repetitive activities, and absence spells. The report said that the behavioral changes were believed to be secondary to schizophrenia. The neurologist followed up and pointed to the fact that Sarah had both auditory and visual hallucinations during differing hospital visits. Her thoughts were Autism, and rule out schizophrenia; that required an inpatient stay in the psychiatric unit. Sarah went straight from the video EEG to the inpatient unit at Mayo. The referring doctor granted liberal visiting privileges. The long halls and underground tunnels finally took us to the unit. It was the longest walk of my life. My husband and I were very scared for our daughter.

Once at the unit they gave me paperwork, and so I sat there not really filling it out. My husband sat with our daughter in the room that would be hers. I went to that room after I managed to finish a portion of the paper work. Sarah was being shown where to put her stuff, and the button she needed to push if she needed help. I knew that she would not push the button if she needed help, and would probably end up hurting herself. Therefore, I mentioned that it might not be a good idea to leave Sarah with them. She did not function at an independent level, and I felt unsure that any in the unit possessed an awareness of her difficulties. Surprise at my desire to take her home, the nurse told me that someone would be sitting by Sarah's door all night; that offered a bit of relief for me. After getting Sarah ready for bed, we left, and then I cried. The dark consumed me as we went to our hotel. Once there, exhaustion hardly resulted in sleep. I should have been able to sleep for days, but it did not come. I sat upon the couch weeping, not able to stop. I felt I was not low enough so I fell to my knees in silent prayer, pouring myself out to my Lord. I told Him how I was failing my daughter, because my best was not good enough. I asked Him to let her know that at least He was there—in any way that she could understand. My prayers became actual groans as my cries shook my entire body. I could not get low enough, as I lay completely on the floor. My entire being was broken, and in the morning, I noticed that the left side of my face had literally fallen or drooped.

Sarah's stay at the unit was difficult. An understanding of what to expect of her under her more normal circumstances needed to be provided. I became her interpreter for that endeavor. Her communicative abilities, her food peculiarities, and her abilities to function in everyday life were a mystery for them. The unit's rules included the practice of good nutrition, which usually makes sense for everybody. With Sarah, even under normal circumstances we never made her drink milk, because she had some allergic response to it. She only recently expanded her abilities in eating a wider variety of foods. Under her more recent and troubling circumstances, she hallucinated while she ate and that caused conflict and an inability to eat. For this particular time in the unit, teaching good nutrition might contribute to more conflict in Sarah's eating experience. Eating something she found appetizing, in the absence of conflict would have been a victory; journal episodes allude to that.

The professionals asked what I had come to understand about all the conflict. What about the cast members? I made sense of it to the following degree: Mr. Toad, Getty, and Mr. Winky are characters in movies that Sarah used to love watching. They were either good or bad, mostly according to Sarah's determination on any particular day. Her preoccupations with the movies and the characters in them morphed into actual real life preoccupations and then hallucinations. Not so hard to comprehend when one considers the fact that normal people draw from the fabric of all they take in when experiencing hallucinations. Perhaps I should have been more worried in the summer of 2003, when I found Sarah crying after she independently navigated to a web site about the discontinuation of the Disney Mr. Toad ride. One particular site had Mr. Toad in a casket, dead. It upset her so much—real tears and mourning. Upon seeing it, she cried out to me for comfort. The reason that Sarah sliced her throat with scissors became apparent as well. In the days and weeks that followed she would point to her throat and tell me, "Throat frozen," or, "It's broken." When she did, it caused me to reflect about times before the scissor incident when she told tell me the same thing. The scissor event was the result of Sarah having discomfort in her throat. While she found it offensive enough to do something very nonsensical about it, she did not want to kill herself. She wanted to get rid of the pain or troubling sensation that she was having in her throat.

Interactions with so many nurses and doctors caused me to consider things that might have contributed to Sarah's break into overt signs of psychosis, besides the fact that she was already autistic. The doctors would be considering all probabilities, and that fact caused me to realize the blame could be mine, in their eyes. It was crushing to realize that the doctors might have to consider me as a cause. When I was filling out the forms the night before, so many of the questions alluded toward the differing types of abuses in the history of the patient. In this sort of a backdrop, isn't there always a refrigerator mother or mommy dearest? To some, yes, they cannot help but blame the mom. I had seen this during some years in the school experience, when various professionals would confide to me about things said or considered about me behind my back; one aide quit because of it. Fortunately, considerations were not hidden at Mayo. We ended up having a chance encounter with one of the doctors who initially suspected schizophrenia. I told him outright that I feared that they thought I caused Sarah's issues. Perhaps all the attempts at having her reach her full potential, through more intensive teaching, had become too much of a stress for her. That doctor gave assurance, and talked about the need for diagnostics for identifying Sarah's problems. Another doctor, who would follow Sarah for quite some time to come, let my husband and I know that the blame's focus was not on us. Dr. Lloyd A. Wells turned out to be a blessing for years to come. Through the ensuing years, his empathy and willingness to keep trying provided a sense of calm in our more than occasional storms.

Sarah's newest troubles created a more complicated history, as compared to what autism alone would have represented. The doctors were thorough in their documentations, with the result being that they had seen episodes where Sarah responded to Mr. Winky, Mr. Toad, and Getty. She would get angry, yell, and lash out. They believed her skills diminished, since they improved upon trying different medication. The hallucinations also decreased upon the new medication trial. The doctors ruled out previously tried medications as probabilities for treatment, since they seemed ineffective. Sarah tried Abilify with no result, and then she tried Zyprexa, with Cogentin for side effects. During her stay with them, one test indicated that she is a slow metabolizer of the D26 enzyme, and that causes complications with the administration of certain medications; that would have been useful to know before we started tries in medicating her, since she already tried some of those medications that might cause problems.

Upon Sarah's release from the unit, I felt a bit dismayed because she was not herself yet. I was not ready to entertain the notion that this would be who she was for quite some time to come. Therefore, I kept journal notes about her episodes in the hopes that the light bulb would come on at any time for anyone! As if, the journaling would be a precursor to some sort of miracle. Perhaps the light bulb needed to come on for me, since I kept insisting on that miracle. We saw the outpatient psychiatrist about a week after discharge from the unit. We reported that the aggression stopped, but Sarah still did not eat or go to the bathroom on her own. The doctor noted that she still responded to internal stimuli. We expressed concern with the fact that her daily living skills did not improve to the level of former function and the doctor shared our concern. We talked at length and decided to give the medication a little more time to do some good, especially since the aggression towards others was gone. I gave the doctor updates with assurance that she received them. She always got in touch with us, when needed.

Sarah continued on the Zyprexa (z) and Cogentin (c) for the months that followed. For a short time, we tried some Buspar (b) alongside the other two medications, but that appeared to make Sarah worse.

Two Months to May
- *(2/18/04) Sarah continues to have conflict with Getty. She continues to be zombie like at times throughout the day. She continues to have problems while eating. She continues to have confusion while using the bathroom. Instead of going pee, she stands up, confused about the process. She has started standing,*

facing a wall (right up to it) and chanting again. She has started some weird head movements again. z,c

- *(2/23/04) Sarah is becoming violent like back in late December. Today she started having conflict within herself and seemed to be having auditory hallucination. She became more and more worked up. She screamed incessantly and then kicked with her feet and slammed with her hands, the dashboard of the truck. She started hitting me. She opened the glove compartment and threw items at me. This went on during very busy traffic as I was picking my son up from high school. I parked in a secluded spot when I got to the high school. I needed to give her time to come down from her episode. I do not like the judging people do when this sort of thing is happening. She came down enough to remorsefully cry and tell me she was sorry and held her arms out for a hug. She also said, "Turn it off," and I think she was asking me to stop the noise in her head because the truck radio was already off. z,c,b*
- *(2/25/04) Sarah went up to her uncle, and hit and kicked him even though he had nothing to do with telling her she could not have a 7-up. As a matter of fact, he had made cookies special for her to eat and had given her some right before. She would not cease going after her uncle. I had noticed before this she was revving up for an episode. As I tried to stop her from going after her uncle, she grabbed my hair. I held her wrists and continually told her, "Sarah let go of my hair. You are hurting me. This is not good." She would not let go of my hair. This went on for a few minutes. She never did let go. I had to pry her fingers, that my hair was wrapped around. She continued to be inconsolable for ten minutes or so but did finally calm down. z,c,b*
- *(2/26/04) Sarah had a hard time this morning. She would be screaming out of the blue because of what was going on in her head. No outward event was causing it. This went on frequently. z,c,b*
- *(3/3/04) For the past few days, Sarah continues to scream or cry at times because of things going on in her head. She continues to have conflict and asks for help because of what*

is going on in her head. Sarah does things like ask for a movie, and then when it starts, she turns it off and starts crying asking us to turn it back on. Another example is that while Sarah is putting on her shoes to go somewhere she is being told by whatever is going on in her head, "Sarah, take your shoes off." I know because she said it aloud, an existing habit of echoing what she hears. Sarah asks for some sort of food and then she is not able to eat because of whatever is going on in her head. If she communicates that she needs help to eat then we help and she is able to eat. Sarah continues to head up the stairs even though she does not want to. She ends up standing facing the wall and screaming, if she ends up in her room upstairs. She will ask for help when this happens, and we take her hand, and then she doesn't go up the stairs. Sometimes if she did not ask for help, and we did not see that it was going on, she would end up in her room very distressed in the position previously mentioned. z,c,b

- (4/2/04) She was hallucinating more, but there seemed to be less aggression. This afternoon she started incessantly giggling (loudly) for more than ten minutes. I have been coaching her when she does this and telling her that it is "too much", and she seems to respond by toning it down a bit. She just seemed like someone who was giddy from drinking. She then began to demand something that we would not be able to do. She knew that we would not be able to do it. She began hitting on my son, probably because he had to intervene as we were in the car driving and he did not want her acting out and causing a wreck. She would not allow for his reasoning at the time, even as she has shown herself to be capable of being agreeable on recent occasions. She then began to rage by screaming for quite a long time. She was beside herself. She began to rage with things by banging some objects and started to hit me but, I asked her not to hit and she stopped. She allowed for a hug at some point and calmed as I hugged her. Afterward she remained very disconnected in her actions whether it was trying to attend to a movie or to a physical activity. She could not focus at all. She seemed to be having auditory hallucinations. She has been *having visual hallucinations too. Of note, we had a very active morning that Sarah seemed to enjoy. We went to Chuck E Cheese, a movie and the library. All things she looks forward to and should enjoy. z,c*

By late April, I told the doctor that Sarah did not engage in extreme violence. We redirected her about not using physical force, and she accepted correction. Screaming out of the blue seemed to have ceased, but some of her hallucinatory characters remained present. I seemed to be a good guy, and Steve was big and strong with an ability to defeat her hallucinatory characters by simply invoking the fact that he was big and strong. The hallucinations did not seem as frequent. Sarah was able to eat and use the bathroom without help. Watching TV still brought conflict. She constantly hugged me and smelled my face for comfort. Sarah started going on outings with the in-home therapists, and after her success during outings, she started some of her academics with them. We looked forward to a pleasant summer of fun outings with a little emphasis on teaching.

In-Home Journal Entry
(5/13/04) We did Appetease, trampoline, journal, conversation and math. Jana came with us to Appetease. Sarah sat nicely and waited for Jana and me to finish our ice cream as she had already finished. We really tried to focus on doing more structured work the last 45 minutes. Sarah is getting a little better at sitting longer again. That was the main focus, to finish several tasks before leaving the table. (April)

During an office visit in May, we reported a bit more improvement to the psychiatrist. The times when Sarah experienced internal conflict that resulted in agitation were few and she allowed for redirection when they happened. She continued her activities of in-home tutoring and outdoor recreation. The doctor noted significant weight gain in a short amount of time, about 18 pounds in approximately three months. Being aware of how physically active we kept Sarah, it was easily determined that the weight gain most probably was a side effect of the Zyprexa. We needed to consider switching medications. Therefore, Geodon was the next choice.

In the summer of 2004, we took the boat out a lot. Sarah loved to go tubing! I remember being on the beach one time with her. We were resting on blankets and waiting for the boat. She was doing well, being patient, and enjoying the sun. But seasons change, and in a little while it would be fall, and then it would be winter.

၅

Other 2004 Episodes

- *(1/10/04) Jaw locking. Confusion while eating. Head prone backwards with arms up. r*
- *(1/16/04) We are happy. Sarah, Jana and I are driving through McDonald's to get breakfast. I hand out the food. We are driving down the road. Sarah screams a high pitched scream. She throws her food. She spits food out of her mouth. She is very angry. She is hitting the seat. She is angry like this for less than a minute. She puts her arms up as if she is a prisoner in the back seat. She cries. She cannot eat because her arms are up. She will not put them down. She tells me her back hurts. That goes on until we get home. We are home. I put the food on the table. Sarah asks for the food but will not eat it. The food stays on the table. She is not going to eat it. s*
- *(1/20/04) Sarah kicks the TV for no apparent reason (not due to what is on as it is Veggie Tales). Sarah scratches on the leather furniture and screams at Getty. "Sarah we have to Getty's closet," she says. z*
- *(2/23/04) These continue to go on daily: zoning out, hallucinating visually and auditorily, screaming out of the blue with no outward trigger, not eating on own, still confused with going potty, eyes tearing without crying. Some other instances: At Chuck E Cheese, she was bending down and picking up things that were not there. She also aggressively moved towards, and then hit a game that two little girls were playing. While watching Veggie Tales she was screaming and becoming distressed. While*

Ann Dunham

walking to Sinclair for a treat she was arguing with what she was hearing in her head.

- (3/4/04) She just beat the crap out of me. I do not know how to defend myself because I do not want to hurt her. She is so remorseful and pale after the fact. She keeps asking me to help her. This episode lasted for twenty to thirty minutes. She was having a lot of problems with the conflict in her head previous to this, she was closing her eyes and chanting. What precipitated the event? Nothing that does not happen at least a dozen times a day. I told her she could not have another cookie. She started becoming agitated, disorganized in her actions, rummaging through cupboards in the kitchen. I was trying to redirect her and accidentally stepped on her recently stubbed toe. Then she came after me, caught a bunch of my hair in her hand, and started trying to bite me, sock me, and even spit at me. She has never spit at me, ever. After the episode, she sat very spacey, eyes watering but not crying and would intermittently rock her head back and forth. z,b,c

- (3/11/04) Sarah screams out. No outward trigger is observable. She still has the voice (or thought) that is telling her to "Go upstairs," or telling her whatever she does that she enjoys doing is "bad." She will still ask to watch a movie and then scream as she turns it off, because she does not want to turn it off. Same old conflict thing. This stuff happens more than just occasionally. She has hit on occasion, but I have been able to tell her not to do it, and she is not into the marathon aggression that she was getting into before. At times, she is doing weird things with her mouth, like a marionette doll. She still has the times when she is fending off the negative stuff by closing her eyes and chanting. The past couple of nights I noticed her doing the thing where she positions her head backwards and sideways (perhaps involuntary). She has had instances where one minute she is profusely giggling and then the next minute she is unresponsive. Before Sept 2003 she used to have giggling fits. Since she was really little, in fact. It had stopped at some point and it is curious to see it back. z,b,c

143

- *3/15/04: Sarah wet her pants yesterday. Not typical of her. She did not even wet her pants when she ended up with interstitial cystitis. Sarah had a very rough Sunday. Disconnected in her actions. She became angry or violent over popcorn even as we told her she could have some. The conflict came no matter what we did or said. She physically attacked whoever was in her path. I tried the extra med (as needed) during one episode and it did not have a calming effect. About twenty minutes after I gave it to her, she began screaming due to what she was hearing in her head. Then she was crying and lashing out. A rough cycle of emotions. She had some weird movements of her head, one time it was quite a violent unexpected movement. z,b,c*

Chapter 11: The Grandest Redirect

Waiting for her to get better, 2004 (eleven and twelve years old). Another office visit occurred in September. The general agreement was that Sarah continued to make some progress. While the doctor visited with Sarah, she noted better cooperation and ability to follow directions. She also noted the absence of aggression and only one period of hallucinating that might be pretend play. We decided to put off public school placement, and to continue with the tutoring from the individuals who taught our in-home program. Sarah's auditory defensiveness to do with the PA systems, and her general inability to tolerate the school environment, remained concerning. Unfortunately, even with the Geodon seemingly responsible for continued good progress, the weight gain continued. She was at 134 pounds, a 16 pound weight gain in about four months. This gain occurred even though we kept her quite active throughout the summer.

We decided to keep her on the Geodon for the next several months, since she had been able to resume normal activities and the aggression had all but stopped. We hoped that she might continue with some forward progress in her tutoring sessions. She loved her time with the gals who did sessions with her. If she continued to do well, she might have been able to participate in some school again. We applied for home schooling for the time being. When we applied, I met with some from the district and they offered to do some functional evaluations of Sarah's levels of performance. Since we felt that the offensiveness of the school environment might be too hard on Sarah, they offered to do the assessments in our home. The district offered integration back into the school environment, whenever we deemed appropriate. At some point, I wanted her to associate with kids she knew from school again, but I needed to see sustained wellness first.

I continued to hope that she was over her worst troubles, and it just seemed prudent to let a little more time pass before she integrated back to public school. For a while longer, Sarah learned from the in-home therapists.

- *(8/5/04) In Math today Sarah corrected herself (without prompt) on a money problem. She realized she was counting wrong on a problem and started over. Then double checked the previous problem and found the same mistake, fixing it as well. She also did an awesome job reading today. (BJ)*
- *(9/20/04) Sarah and I went to McDonald's. Sarah ordered her own food and waited very patiently. We also washed my car. She had the hose and was a lot of help. She got soaked! (Cortney)*
- *(9/21/04) Sarah was kind of spacey at the zoo today. She was doing a lot of repetitive movements. Picking up imaginary stuff off the ground. She had high energy. Sarah did a nice job journaling. At Appetease Sarah kept talking about "no worksheets," so we worked out of the books instead. It kept her a lot more interested than the worksheets. (April)*
- *(9/23/04) Sarah did not want to work when we first got started. She kept trying to play Sonic. She said, "No April. Have to wait. April sit down." Then she threw a tantrum and tried hitting me. I had Sarah write out a schedule and then she did fine. (April)*
- *(10/14/04) Sarah has been working very well the past week. She has not been complaining at all. She has also been a lot better at sitting and concentrating. (April)*
- *(10/04) Tonight I was upset, crying and telling Steve that I am tired of being viewed as an eccentric. Sarah became disturbed. She came to where I was and said, "Momma, why are you crying?" She hugged me and patted me on the back and said, "It's okay, Sarah's here." She started crying because I was so sad. Then we were both all better. (Ann)*

Ann Dunham

Ann & Sarah

Hello, Dr. Wells

From September through October, things went quite a bit better than the previous year. November got a little rougher. In the first part of December, we visited with the outpatient doctor. Sarah's symptoms worsened and the timing coincided with last winter. She engaged in unpredictable aggression, and when we finally identified the triggers, they were nonsensical ones. The doctor noted that Sarah constantly moved during the visit; she responded to simple commands and seemed happy, but she also responded to obvious hallucinations and internal stimuli. There seemed to be a seasonal component to some of her problems. The doctor felt it important to keep the Geodon on board, but we decided to add Luvox very slowly in order to address the seasonal issue. I was to report to the doctor in two weeks, or sooner if things became too difficult. Titrating up would be a long process, so I had this great idea. Let us take Sarah's mind of her troubles and go to Disneyland; the grandest redirect ever!

I kept thinking about how Sarah turned out of the ordinary events into rituals, or repertoires. I redirected her in an effort to break the development of ongoing ritual; the previously mentioned occurrences on the bike path and in the elementary school art class are examples of those redirects. The previous winter had been so rough on her, and I feared her mind's penchant for repeating certain events; I wanted to fill her mind with happy associations from Disneyland so that she might not have negative associations with winter. It seemed important to try. Was it possible to stop or put off this seasonal component to Sarah's problems by distracting her? We would surprise the California grandparents with a short visit, and we would go to Disneyland. Due to Sarah's difficulties we did not fly, instead opting for a road trip. Everyone in the car listened to the same set of songs repeatedly from a CD. We developed a sense of humor about it, as we wanted to keep her at peace. That worked here and there, but eventually she listened to the CD while performing ritual; she manipulated the recordings by pressing play, repeat, and skip a certain way. This made listening to music very difficult for Sarah. A video player in the car also started to cause the same kind of conflict and eventual frustration for Sarah. She did not find enjoyment in these rituals, they angered her. We all held our chin up anyway because we were going to Disneyland! We kept driving in order to reach a Del Taco on our first day, because that was the first great reinforcer for the trip. She remembered Del Taco from when we lived in the desert and she was excited to get a frosty and fries.

We actually arrived in a state with a Del Taco on the first night. After eating, we found a hotel. At some point the next morning, we let Sarah swim because she did not back down about it. We needed to break into the pool for her swimming time; it was a neat indoor pool. After that, we made a quick getaway because we wanted to get to Whiskey Petes. The biggest thing to remember about Whiskey Petes is the roller coaster, and Sarah stated her mission when we arrived; she was gung-ho to get on Desperado. I rode on it several years previous with my brother, and I could not bring myself to get on that roller coaster again. Steve and Jeff endured the ride with Sarah, and afterward they joked about the need to change their underwear. The neat thing about that day was that hardly anyone was there. We did not need to wait in line for any of the rides or attractions. Who goes to State Line in the middle of the week in the middle of winter anyway? Sarah enjoyed herself. It was so slow there that we took a chance and actually ate in one of the restaurants with Sarah. She did okay. After a good nights rest and breakfast, we left for our main destination. California here we come.

We made a stop before the grandparents. My best friend lived in the town right before theirs. I had missed Kaye terribly, but she would hardly know because I really withdrew after Sarah's worsening. We went over to her parents' house first. I held them in high esteem for their beautiful consistencies and the ways in which they contributed to the well being of others around them. After I knocked on the door, Kaye's father answered and then he just started laughing; his face lit up. I had not affected anyone that way in a long time! He gave Kaye a call and told her to come over, but he did not tell her why. As she came pulling up from where she lived down the road, she expected that her mom or dad was in need of some help. She curiously looked at our car with the out of state plates and while approaching the steps she made sense of it all. Ann was in town and that meant it was time to go to Del Taco! We cried, talked, laughed, hugged, and ate. It was like a mini reunion and it meant so much to me. I consider Kaye and her friendship to be one of the best things that ever happened to me. Let this be memorial to that fact!

We surprised the two sets of grandparents in much the same way. Steve's parents were almost in shock. It had been a while since they saw our kids, because they stayed home caring for another son alongside of whom they needed to remain. We had not been inclined to travel with Sarah during those years as well. Everyone looked a little different, so getting reacquainted took about three seconds! My dad and his wife were thrilled that we made the trip—such a happy surprise. They made one to two trips a year to South Dakota to visit us, so they had a better time recognizing us! It worked out well because at night, Steve, Jeff, and Jana stayed with Steve's parents and Sarah and I stayed with my dad. My dad and his wife missed the opportunity to see more of Jeff and Jana, but they were so good about it. I love them for not making too much of the fact. Dad had a room at his place that was totally blacked out at night, allowing Sarah to get a really good night's sleep. Sarah spent days at Steve's parents because their backyard was the desert and you could walk for miles if you wanted. Sarah did not need to walk that far to find a bush to conquer and defeat. She kept finding broken branches with which to attack bushes; she attacked bush after bush after bush after bush...I think you get the point. She compulsively and repetitively bush whacked. After Sarah ran out of bushes to conquer, we left for Disneyland.

The hotel at Disneyland had a huge lobby with lots of windows for check-in, but on the day of our arrival no lines were in sight. Sarah liked spending a little time in hotel stores. We settled in our room quickly, but did not stay there long. We ended up riding a tram to the park and, with Sarah's auditory sensitivities, the constant talking on the overhead speakers made it difficult for her to enjoy. We went from that ride to the little train that goes around quite a bit of the park. Soon enough we ended up at one of the park restaurants, and that represented food heaven to Sarah because of its buffet style—pick now, pay at the end of the line. Once we finished eating, we started moving toward the rides. It was a beautiful day, with hardly any people at the park; we did not wait long to get on most of the rides. It seemed as if the Lord above prescribed these kinds of conditions just for us so that we experienced a great family time at the park.

When mid day approached I started to have concern about Sarah's "all on" status, meaning we were either jogging or running in order to keep up with her as she pursued each adventure. I felt some disappointment toward mid afternoon when it became hard for the rest of us to keep pace with her. Jeff and Jana just kept going with it and never complained. Later in the day, we discovered the California Adventure portion of the park. A few more people had come to play at Disneyland by then. We kept riding the roller coaster in this section for Sarah, but we enjoyed other rides in between. One of the other rides drenched me so I let the kids, Steve, and Sarah go ahead while I looked for something dry to wear in a gift shop. They headed to the roller coaster for another ride. After my purchase from the gift shop, I intended to take a slow walk to the roller coaster; my intention lasted about as long as it took to exit the gift shop door, because I heard Sarah screaming. Even though the roller coaster is quite a distance from the gift shop, I knew that scream anywhere. I started running. I made it to the roller coaster and met my slightly dejected family. My kids told me that some individuals in the line started to taunt Sarah when they realized she struggled with the wait. She lost it and had an episode. We were used to occasional bullying by strangers and almost constant scrutiny by them. Years ago, before I was used to it, I picked a fight with a carnival worker for taunting Sarah. For this time at Disneyland, I followed my kids' example of practicing restraint and we just moved on and tried a couple of the other rides. We figured out it was time to stop for the day and headed to the hotel shortly after that. Everyone was a little worn out.

We needed to get something to eat once back at the hotel and decided to go to Goofy's Kitchen. There was a little entertainment from Disney characters, and Sarah liked getting to see Mickey, Minnie, Goofy, and everyone else. She enjoyed it for a short time, but while eating she started to have conflict, and then she threw up. She then started in on one of her episodes with obvious auditory and visual hallucinations. Whatever her mind was occupied with seemed to give her over to complete torment. Steve wrapped her in his arms and quickly took her to the hotel room so that Jeff, Jana, and I had some time to eat. The unfortunate nature of Sarah's problems made us sad, so we lost our appetite. The person who helped us at our table graciously consoled us, and offered to pack some food for Steve since he had not eaten. Sarah recovered by the time we arrived at the room. We all slept after that. The grand redirect only did so much. It certainly did not stop her hallucinations.

I guess we were glad we tried the trip. It was nice to see the grandparents and friends. I sat there by Sarah in the back seat of the car and looked at the other two kids. How much more character building could they take? The world's sensibilities continually offered the fact that living normal family experience takes precedent over persevering, in a situation such as ours. I guess I might represent a thief who stole normalcy from Jeff and Jana, simply because I did not want to give up on Sarah. My own sensibilities most often considered a never healing wound that our family might carry, if we ever gave up on Sarah; because giving up would cause a kind disintegration, a wounding of our family's fabric. We kept Jeff and Jana from physical harm up to this point. I just kept asking the Lord to turn all things toward His good purpose. Hard as it was to see purpose in the sufferings, I reminded myself that many people suffer daily; we had been appointed as Sarah's family and therefore, we endured alongside her.

Her difficulty with acting out due to inner conflict increased dramatically by January. She screamed horrifically and lashed out in a violent manner, at invisible things. She attempted to play games that she previously enjoyed like Dance, Dance Revolution, and even though she did the steps correctly and was quite successful, she screamed horrifically; the game seemed a form of torture. She ended up lashing out at the Playstation, and she kicked holes in the wall, even while successfully fulfilling the requirement of the game. I explained to the psychiatrist that even if I removed the Playstation, Sarah more than likely would develop this craziness during some other previously enjoyable activity. Reflections of Sarah's more distant past took me to a time before her overt psychotic symptoms, when she was younger. She experienced behavior issues in relation to some Gamecube games. Even if the game itself went well she sometimes screamed and cried. Before Gamecube, when she was even younger, cartoons created the same occasional distress. She whined and worried while watching differing cartoons, even if the episode she watched did not involve conflict. She needed reassurance that everything was okay. These earlier things were ones that I had let go of and forgotten, perhaps because she seemed to get over them, or get better. I did not consider a correlation, or pattern that presented itself each year. I now consider the similarity of her behaviors during those events. Sarah's mind entertained mostly negative or distressful thoughts, while doing something enjoyable; the one instance when things in any activity had gone wrong, or the one episode in any cartoon that was upsetting, mattered the most. The negative event seemed to have stronger control than any positive event as far as her memories were concerned. Said another way, she engaged and acted upon the negative memory repeatedly, whenever she again involved herself in the activity that was associated with the memory. If memory has a pecking order, the negative ones are bigger and stronger that the pleasant ones.

Past and present aside, we determined that the Geodon did not help Sarah. We already started lessening the Luvox dose, because of a suspected effect of increased repetitive body movements and phrases; and it did not help in other areas that we wanted to see improvement in anyway. Sarah's sleep pattern was interrupted by this time, with nights of little to no sleep. Sarah did not show violence toward any of us. It seemed as if we learned how to do this new dance with her. I lamented because I did not know how much more our little girl could take. Disorder of thought was tormenting her, and we were in her hell with her. Refractory was the word of this winter. Nothing gave her peace. I asked the doctors for any kind of man made miracle. I asked them to please make her winter go away.

∾

Chapter 12: Winter

Catatonia, 2005 (twelve years old). The doctors considered my reports on Sarah's newest troubles and asked if I wanted her to come for another stay at the unit. Even though I knew she needed help, her stay with them was so cumbersome the last time, making me hesitant to consider another stay. They were great because they allowed for liberal visiting privileges, but I did not know how useful a stay would be, considering the strain it seemed to put upon the regular order of the unit. When asked about the support system at home, I informed them that Sarah spent some time with two of our in-home program therapists. I was not ready to involve the school district or even the specialty school because the medications did not provide that kind of relief yet. I kept waiting to get the meds right.

(1/22/05) It is Saturday, early afternoon. Jana and I have just been beaten up by Sarah as we were trying to get home from a piano lesson. Sarah was having inner conflict this morning, throughout the morning. She did scream on occasion. The screaming from inner conflict has been going on daily though.

Sarah became angry when I had to leave from a drive thru window before we got our food. I had to leave because she was screaming horrifically and couldn't help herself. She became quite enraged when I couldn't go back for the food as that was already the second time we had tried to go back. The first time she had started screaming as well even as she was getting exactly what she wanted.

Sarah began banging me on the head with her fists and also throwing punches on my back. I told Jana to duck and stay out of it as I didn't want Sarah to start hitting her too. But the more I was getting beat... Jana couldn't help but try and deflect the blows I was receiving. By this time Sarah was pulling my hair as well. I was just trying to get us home so I kept driving. Sarah began to punch Jana in the face and to pull her hair. Now she was beating on both of us as I drove. We were deflecting the blows, just trying to get home. People who were driving alongside us were staring, mortified. I pulled off the road to try and calm Sarah down but she only got more violent. I just wanted to get her home. I began driving again and she was pulling my hair out. She was biting the hair out of my head and even did the same to Jana. It was a very helpless situation.

We made it home and Sarah was still in a rage. Jana was beside herself from being bitten on her arm and punched in the face by Sarah. This was a first for Jana, the worst kind. I told Jana to go straight upstairs and stay away from Sarah. Sarah continued to beat me up and kicked me multiple times over. She hit the TV and pulled it so that it crashed to the floor...

There seemed to be no help for the most current situation. I called 911 just because I did not know what else to do. They told me if I wanted to, I could have the police come and arrest her. I called the unit and they told me the same thing. In my mind if you call the police on a mentally disturbed person, the likelihood is that they will get hurt; it might increase the violence. SWAT teams for psychotic people do not exist. I did not know if the police received training in order to understand, or even know what to do, in a situation such as ours. No response team for this kind of situation existed. I did not want to answer her violence with more violence, because the Lord obviously gave me a heart to practice grace in her situations. Sarah seemed to be in a place of destruction on that day and I desperately wanted relief for her. I sent an SOS via email to all the doctors that treat her at Mayo. After that, I went outside for a break since Sarah calmed down. Our next-door neighbor came to talk to me. She told me that she saw Sarah beating us in the car. I offered for her to come in. She came in to talk to Sarah, and was happy to see her calm and well. She then checked the injuries that Jana and I sustained. I think she understood enough because her son has high functioning autism, but I remain hopeful that their dance remains different from ours. As she ended her visit, I told her we already received word from Dr. Wells and he was preparing for Sarah's stay at the unit. While waiting for her room, I read and prayed. My questions continued to be ones without immediate answers and so went my prayers.

> (1/24/05) To My Husband: As I have told you, the Lord has been quiet on issues of Sarah. Or I have not heard Him. I have not even known how to pray on her issues. I have simply felt that the Lord would have us to do as we are doing and practice a kind of patience and grace with Sarah...I do not know His full will on the matters of Sarah. What is His plan for Sarah? And what do I do so that I walk in His will on her issues? Amen.

At Mayo, the doctors just kept trying. A neurologist report alluded to observations by a nurse and another doctor. The main problems for Sarah seemed to be auditory hallucinations where she engaged in conversations with individuals who were not there, and visual hallucinations that usually resulted in agitation. The doctor noted that a few seconds of non-responsiveness sometimes followed the hallucinations, and then she resumed normal activity. The non-responsiveness needed some investigating; so evaluations for metabolic causes were completed. The doctors considered MRI, but put it off since one happened a year earlier, and was negative. They considered EEG, but felt it too problematic due to Sarah's level of behavioral function at the time. Continued tries at medicating remained the biggest recommendation after she had been gone over by the neurologist.

During an Occupational Therapy evaluation, Sarah hated classical music playing in the background. Sarah hates sound with too much treble quality. The OT felt it important to find music that she could enjoy, however all that she experienced turned into conflict, so that not even music soothed her. The OT noted that we already utilized strategies at home such as swimming and swinging, exclusively doing so because Sarah usually responded to favorably to them. The report gave a very long and excellent list of ideas for settling at night, but the active hallucinations and manias cared little for such a list. I previously had exposure to, and understood, the OT's suggestions since Sarah lived her entire life in the world of autism. Everyone tried so hard to help, but the fact for the current time was that we were not dealing with anything near normal, and Sarah was not responding to most of these types of interventions normally. Her world represented an upside down one. Things considered soothing by many, became intolerable for Sarah.

Another therapist wanted to help Sarah to utilize certain relaxation techniques. Mostly, breathing exercises and music. The deliberate breathing required repetition, or ritual. How could I explain to the therapist that this meditative breathing might be bad? Ritual proved harmful to Sarah, and the repetitive breathing might contribute to future absence spells. Past absence spells disturbed her enough to result in violence and/or screaming. Music and repetition (rote) agitated her. Sarah tried relaxation with the therapist, and she engaged in the deliberate breathing, but she looked disturbed; the way she usually looked when dealing with internal conflict. Sarah's thought processes were fried, and that made repetition of any sort an enemy. Meditation upon meaningless music, breathing, or idle thinking was in vain. It really pointed to her susceptibility toward spells, as compared to some individual's susceptibility to hypnotizing. Perhaps Sarah's involvement in any sort of repetition put her in a trance state, without benefit of suggestion from the hypnotist. All she had was her inner conflict from which to draw.

As crazy as Sarah's world was, it took some days to be revealed to those at the unit. The doctors and professionals did not yet completely realize the extent of Sarah's torment. I despaired because as much as I tried to explain it, words did not do it justice. I read in the Psalms a lot. I made the Psalmist's prayers my prayers for Sarah's situation. One afternoon, I prayed until I wept and soon after I fell asleep. The next day, Sarah experienced an episode like many I previously tried to explain. Being witness to the episode offered all at the unit a clearer perspective, and I felt the hand of God because my prayer the day before was that the doctors' eyes might witness the ongoing and crushing torment from which she suffered. Confirmation that He heard my prayer came later in the day, when I received a call from one of the unit professionals. She said exactly this: "We needed to see that to understand," and she told me that they would make sure the doctors knew about what happened to Sarah, and the fact that medication did not yet give her relief. Sarah had a little better time after her episode that day, but did not settle to sleep until very late.

Her lack of sleep amazed the professionals at the unit, since a double dose of one sedative medication, and a dose of Thorazine did not cause her to fall asleep. They gave her those medications to bring her down, but no sedation occurred. The next morning, Sarah had another episode. Obviously none of the medications they tried for calming her helped. The doctors simply continued their tries at medicating Sarah. They tried Clonidine, but without benefit. Thorazine was tried for several days without sustained relief, so the doctors brought Depakote on board along with Risperdal. Sarah started to show less aggression and displayed fewer outbursts. She also became a little more social. They discontinued the Thorazine and left her on Depakote and Risperdal.

The doctors talked about Sarah having a rare variant of periodic catatonia, in context of the autism. Ativan was the treatment of choice for that. When they gave Sarah the Ativan along with the other medications, she showed even more improvement. Catatonia seemed to be the main nature of Sarah's difficulties, and relapse remained a strong possibility; but she seemed better for the time being. The doctors discharged her during the second week in February. Her diagnoses were Autism, Psychosis NOS, and chronic mental illness. The GAF upon admission was 25 and upon release, 45. We decided to pursue genetic aspects with the doctors at Mayo on our next visit.

In the middle of March, Sarah had a follow up visit with her outpatient psychiatrist. We told the doctor that Sarah had a problem with constant hunger. Weight became a major issue, since Sarah now weighed 151 pounds; about a 10 pound gain since her release from the unit in February. We thought Sarah was more manageable, but she did not engage in her usual activities and she still seemed to hear voices actively. The doctor noted that Sarah did not attend to questions directed towards her. She also felt that Sarah seemed agitated, hyperactive, and in need of constant redirection. Sarah was on so many medications; Depakote, Risperdal, Ativan, and Cogentin. We discussed the multiple medications and decided to get her off the Ativan, because it is not for long-term use. The Depakote and Risperdal remained weight gain culprits, so we needed to address that concern. The plan was to slowly taper the Ativan down, to final discontinuation; and then we planned to taper the Depakote in the same way. After the visit with the psychiatrist, we followed up with Genetics.

During our conversation with the doctors in genetics, they noted that Sarah had many behavior issues. We shared a couple of things with the geneticist. We told them that Sarah developed a good attention span from both preschool and in-home teaching. She sustained that improvement up to about the middle of first grade. From then on, things proved to be up and down; with significant worsening at the time that she developed overt signs of psychosis in fourth grade. From the middle of first grade to forth grade, attending to things at school was not as successful as attending to things she enjoyed at home. She most enjoyed illustrating characters from cartoons and video games, but her ability to do these drawings ceased upon her initial worsening. Sarah started to have bladder issues in third grade and a doctor identified interstitial cystitis as the cause. She experienced problems with constipation at about the same time. We felt that Sarah displayed clumsiness that she did not have in her earlier years. Her muscle tone and strength seemed diminished, even as she engaged in more activity than most. Sarah did not seem to have problems with worrisome weight gain until starting meds. When she did not eat enough in her earliest years, she maintained a seventy-fifth percentile for weight, even though she was quite active.

Ann Dunham

Weight Chart

Age	Weight	Difference	Comment	Source	Approx per year weight gain
0	8 lbs3 oz				
I					
2 yrs 10 mos	33 lbs				
3 yrs 7 mos	34.3 lbs	1.3 lbs increase		Dr. Blake	1.3 lbs
4 yrs 4 mos	38.5 lbs	4.2 lbs increase		Dr. Blake	I 4.2 lbs
5 yrs 3 mos	43.25 lbs	4.75 lbs increase		Dr. Blake	4.75 lbs
6 yrs I mos	48 lbs	4.75 lbs increase		Dr. Blake	I 4.75 lbs
7 yrs 4 mos	57.25 lbs	9.25 lbs increase		Dr. Blake	9.25 lbs
8 yrs 4 mos	64.5 lbs	7.25 lbs increase		Dr. Blake	7.25 lbs
9 yrs 10 mos	88.25 lbs	23.75 lbs increase		Dr. Blake	23.75 lbs
10 yrs 3 mos	92.25 lbs	4 lb increase		Dr. Blake	4 lbs
II yrs I mos	104.28 lbs	12.03 lbs increase	Started meds	Mayo (neuro) I/27/04	12.03 lbs
II yrs 2 mos	99.65 lbs	4.63 lbs decrease		Mayo (peds) 2/3/04	
II yrs 2 mos	99.65 lbs	Same		Mayo (psych) 2/II/04	
II yrs 5 mos	118.4 lbs	18.65 lbs increase	Zyprexa	Mayo (psych) 5/25/04	
II yrs 9 mos	134 lbs	15.6 lbs increase	Geodon	Mayo (psych) 9/14/04	
12 yrs 2 mos	141.5 lbs	6.5 lbs increase	Depakote, Risperdal	Mayo (psych) 2/9/05	38.22 lbs
12 yrs 3 mos	151.1 lbs	9.9 lbs increase	Depakote, Risperdal	Mayo (psych) 3/14/05	
14 yrs 7 mos	158.8 lbs	7.7 lbs increase	Lithium, Depo, Risperdal	Mayo (psych) 7/5/07	
14 yrs 9 mos	160.6 lbs	2.2 lbs increase	Lithium, Depo, Risperdal	Mayo (psych) 9/7/07	19.I lbs
15 yrs	167.2 lbs	6.4 lbs increase	Lithium, Depo, Risperdal	Mayo (psych) 12/10/07	
15 yrs 6 mos	176 lbs	8.8 lbs increase	Lithium, less risperdal	Mayo (psych) 6/2/08	
15 yrs 9 mos	179.5 lbs	2.5 lbs increase	Lithium, less risperdal	Mayo (psych) 9/2/08	18.9 lbs

Tests that the genetic doctors completed during the most
recent inpatient stay at the unit follow: plasma amino acid profile,
ceruloplasmin, homocysteine, vitamin B12, folic acid, pipecolic acid,
urine organic acids, unrinalysis, T4, TSH, ECG, ammonia, CBC, and
electrolytes. Those were all within normal range. Fragile X testing in
1995 was negative, but the geneticist decided to repeat that test. They
wanted an ophthalmology evaluation. They also wanted to review MRI
and CT scans previously done. Audiometric testing was called for due
to Sarah's hearing sensitivities. A 600 band stage chromosome analysis
as part of a chromosomal microarray, was sent off to Texas. The
chromosomal microarray testing reported an absence of deletions
or duplications in around sixty different regions; that type of testing
does not pick up imprinting abnormalities or uniparental disomy. That
being the case, they wanted to arrange a methylation study to look for
abnormalities consistent with Prader-Willi or Angelman syndromes.
Sarah was negative for Rett mutation. They wanted to perform a
free and total carnitine and acylcarnitine profile because of Sarah's
muscle weakness. A check on lactate and pyruvic acid and ammonia
was suggested as well. I felt encouraged because the doctors worked
so hard on Sarah's behalf; nevertheless, the visit needed to end early
because she kept having episodes. We headed to the lab for blood
work, but that did not work out either. We left without completing
the blood work, and that was discouraging.

After the March visit with the doctor, we slowly tapered off the
Ativan. We started to slowly taper down the Cogentin, which put
off side effects, and Sarah began doing things that may or may not
have been associated with side effects of Risperdal. I reported the
concern of questionable side effects from Risperdal to the doctor.
Due to that possibility of side effects, we brought the Cogentin back
on board. During this time, Sarah engaged in a tremendous amount of
chanting and body movements of a repetitive nature, in certain areas
of the house. When she came out of the episodes, she usually became
violent or angry and very seldom was she peaceful. She also refused
to enter certain rooms in the house, and was not able to move
about normally, similar to the progression in the fall of 2003 before
we tried any medications. I asked the doctors if it was time to taper

and discontinue the Risperdal, because Sarah received no sustainable benefit from being on it. The dose schedule might have been the biggest factor for that failure.

> *(4/19/05) Sarah is becoming less able to settle in the evenings. Doing the repetitive chanting and body movements a lot in the evenings which used to be the quieter time for Sarah. We have been getting into a lot more physical activity like bike rides and walking. While doing these activities which Sarah considers fun, the repetitive body movements and chanting are present. As I type this Sarah has just had an episode and is now acting out with tremendous anger and some violence.*

By the last part of April, Sarah was almost completely off the Risperdal. She had a tremendous amount of episodes—repetitive body movements with chanting, followed by laughter, or more predominantly anger and violent outburst. She had a lot of the internal conflict with all the usual suspects. Certain words triggered episodes. One day, we rode our tandem bike by the school when the PE teacher said "hurry" to some of the kids who were running. Sarah heard him say hurry and she engaged in an episode while on the bike, hard but doable for her. The phrase "there you are" also triggered episodes, and that was seen at the unit during the last visit. As May ensued, Sarah still refused to enter certain rooms in the house: the kitchen, downstairs bathroom and hall, living room, and basement. She developed chanting and body movements as a prerequisite for going to the bathroom, going upstairs, and going out the front door. She really only liked leaving the house through the garage. She hit me once when I could not fix something (that was not fixable), but overall she seemed more able to follow directives and accept correction, when compared to worse times.

> *(5/4/05) While at my mom's today, Sarah was playing with the hose, which has become known as an "evil water snake hose." She usually would have a great time watering the trees, grass and dandelions. She seems to always have a lot of imaginary stuff going on, but today it was quite distressing as she was very much into the*

*repetitive nature of what she was doing with the hose. She would
hold the hose in her mouth, sideways, while needing to do her body
movements and chants. She began to get angrier and finally was
quite beside herself with screaming. She came inside and went to
the bathroom, still very angry. She hit the medicine cabinet, me, and
then the door as we left.*

*She also hit my son for no apparent reason after she came out
of an episode in the car. She had an episode in the middle of a
busy intersection while we were on a bike ride. We were trying to
cross the intersection and I said, "Hurry," (darn it), there came the
episode. It happened right when all these soccer moms are trying to
get their kids to the field.*

Sarah had an episode with one of the gals who took her on outings,
just a couple of days after fighting with the evil water snake hose.
Sarah and April frequently visited the zoo together, so reasons for
enjoyment outweighed reasons for aggression. Nevertheless, on the
ride home from the zoo, Sarah had weirdness to do with her seat belt;
she was taking it off and putting it on, then taking it off. April chose to
ignore the behavior, because over the years of working with Sarah she
developed discernment in choosing the battles. For this particular day,
April did not get to ignore the battle, because even in the absence of
correction attempts, Sarah lost it. What happened in the car to April
was similar to what happen back in January 2005 to Jana and me. April
saw that Sarah was hallucinating, and she got the crap beat out of her
while it went on. They were lucky to get home safely. Suffice it to say,
no more outings.

Sarah started a try on Strattera toward the middle of May, but
Depakote remained on board. Upon beginning the newest medication
trial, Sarah continued having all the usual problems. I noted that she
also started to have tremors in her right arm, and head from time
to time; and that had been present for a while before the Strattera.
She started to show confusion when coming out of her episodes.
After one particularly long and rough episode at home, she displayed

confusion about what meal time it was, and seemed to be treating a past memory as a current one. She asked about going to get a happy meal toy as if she had not already gotten it; but she had. Sarah ended up back at the unit due to, "…worsening behaviors, aggression toward parents, and apparent worsening psychosis for possible ECT." The psychiatrist's report noted that significant medication adjustment had transpired within the past months.

Doctor Summary: …During these episodes she is out of it and her mother is unable to redirect. She talks in different voices and repeats certain phrases. She will chant, then become very angry, then chant again. Sometimes this will last a few minutes, sometimes up to 45 minutes. They have noticed certain triggers, one of which is the word "hurry." Usually she is alert afterwards. However, today her mother states that she was quite confused afterwards (an episode) and called her "Rose" (nurse at the unit) and was talking about things "that happened in the past" (at unit confrontation). She also struck out and tried to hit her mother. She had an episode during the interview, where she had repetitive left arm movements, swinging it from side to side rhythmically. She then started talking in two voices, one very low and one which sounded like her usual voice. She did seem to repeat the word "hurry" a few times. She stared at the floor the entire time. This lasted 1–2 minutes, and then the patient returned to playing with the ball. Doctor is in contact with the patient's mother on a regular basis and was apparently concerned about the possible continuous psychosis as well as her lack of response to multiple medication trials. Per her notes, she is considering a trial of ECT. The patient's mother is aware of this, though she states she would like to give the Strattera a trial because it seems to be helping…

From the beginning, the doctors had told me that it takes time for medications to work, sometimes months. I guess I wanted to try the Strattera a little longer because I did not understand ECT; it frightened me, but Sarah's lack of response to medications left no other option but ECT. As with anything, I found arguments for and against this type of treatment, and I considered both sides. Then, I lamented privately in the hotel for the entire night before her first ECT treatment. The first treatment happened right before the weekend, and Sarah continued with her episodes through that ensuing weekend. The long episodes usually resulted in violence. The only identifiable triggers were certain areas of the halls in the unit, but her episodes also happened in other contexts. Saturday's episode resulted in some hitting of staff and seclusion. Sunday was a little better, since Sarah moved herself to her room instead of having to forcibly be taken to the seclusion room. She had episodes both days until wearing herself out, usually around midnight. Monday, as I sat with her after her morning ECT, she briefly chanted and then smacked a book that she had in front of her. She also engaged in a very brief breathing episode, but came out of it fine; a movement of touching her eyes accompanied the breathing one. I did not completely understand what the doctors expectations were at this point, as I had thought we were targeting the repetitive episodes. She was not improving, if that was the sole target.

I took Sarah on a mid day outing after she had been in the unit a few days, having treatments. She engaged in episodes from time to time. Two were distressing, but short-lived, and they did not result in actual violence. The other episodes that were not distressing lasted for various amounts of time. It seemed liked Sarah was trying to stop from doing them on some occasions. I took Sarah on an outing the evening of the next day, and she had a non-violent episode. She only mentioned one bad character. We stayed out for four hours. Upon her return to the unit, she did two rather long repetitive chanting, body movement sessions in differing halls and then returned to her room. After doing that she sat at her desk, kind of spacey and not really responsive. She put on her PJs and went to bed. She said she was ready to go to sleep.

Sarah came home after the first few treatments. We wanted to do the rest on an outpatient basis. The first day back had all the usual suspects but no violence. We drove to the outpatient treatment the next day, and the trip there and back went pretty well. That would not last though.

(5/20/05) When we arrived home, Sarah sat quietly for a while and then she went out back to play with the hose and watch me clean the pool. As she played with the hose, she was quite manageable and did not get into any of the evil water snake hose scenes. Eventually she swam and held great attention to this activity for over an hour (unheard of). Either Steve or I were out with her during that time. She got out of the pool to rest, but then wanted to get back in. Sarah and her father were swimming, having a good time, but then she went to a certain spot in the pool and broke into one of her repetitive vocalizations and body movements in the pool. It went on for a very long time and she ended up screaming and hitting the metal pool side. She hit me as we tried to calm her from the repetitive activity. We were trying to stop her because the activity was alarming and she seemed tormented, along with the fact that she could cause injury to herself. This incident was similar in intensity to the one that happened between Sarah and Heather last Saturday at the unit. Sarah was calm for the rest of the day after this episode.

It seemed clear that Sarah was not heading toward improvement, but there were still quite a few more sessions of ECT to have. Full course had not been determined. I planned to keep making the trips with Sarah for outpatient treatment. Even with all that had transpired; the predominant thought that occupied my mind was that we needed a different place to live, if this was how it was going to be. Most of our neighbors knew us, and watched Sarah have many positive experiences throughout her earliest years. They had seen the many therapists come in and out—those happy days of moving forward and seeing purpose in our endeavors. The neighbors witnessed something a bit different for the past couple years—a not so improved Sarah. New people were moving in and did not understand our challenge. For all they knew, we were abusing our child. That is what it sounded like anyway. How long before the police showed up at our front door? How could I blame anyone for calling the cops, if they did? For many months, I had been driving out to the rural areas with Sarah just to fill the hours. Even if she was suffering, I hoped the movement and change in scenery meant a little something to her. I would drive and imagine a place for Sarah. A place of peace and rest where enduring the scrutiny of others would not be required. Her problems were bad enough, but the added element of misinformed scrutiny was becoming the nail in the coffin. How was it that she and we should be judged by strangers so regularly, while they went about their barely informed business? Truth be told, it seemed as if some friends were also beginning to give the sideways glances—the ones that implied it has to be something that was being done wrong by the family. I used to judge like them before I had Sarah. Being mother to this child, I felt as if I had become a woman without a country and this feeling was of little consequence. What seemed worthy and eternally consequential, was to walk the valleys and climb toward the mountaintops with her, doing so a day at a time. This became the understanding in our family. Between the Lord and I was this request, "Could we have a place for Sarah where her beautiful spirit could shine through the clouds of her illness?"

Apparently, the Lord had considered all of my supplications about a place set apart for Sarah—a beautiful place where the house could be in the very middle of acre upon acre—an impossible dream. I even told Jana and Jeff one time that I wanted a place for Sarah where she could have her own trails to walk about, like the park paths in the city. Damn the hurtful scrutiny of others, bless Sarah! Thus began a purpose that was different, one that would endure alongside a hurting spirit, and accept any outcome.

⚬~⚬

Chapter 13: A Place for Sarah

ECT, 2005 (12 years old). A couple of months before the ECT I knew we would need a place to endure alongside Sarah. That gave our infinite drives on the rural roads more purpose. I was always seeking while driving. One morning, right before one of those drives, I was scanning the newspaper and an ad jumped out—"...one-hundred and sixty acres for auction." My immediate impression was this land would suit Bret's purpose. We knew him from church and he wanted land for ministry. The acreage was entirely too big for our more private need. I cut out the ad and handed it to Steve as he left for church with Jeff and Jana. Sarah and I went for one of our drives, while all the rest were at Sunday service. We were still driving when I received a call from Steve. He was excited about the acreage mentioned in the ad. I was a little surprised that he had investigated the acreage. I was skeptical that the excitement was more about dreaming than actual reality. I resisted checking it out because it was too big.

It was either the same day, or the following one when Steve drove us out to the land. We proceeded down the long drive and through the grove. The trees, creeks and gentle slopes created a visual melody. It was open and large, yet it also provided seclusion and protection. It was what I had imagined aloud to my family, and it was for Sarah. "This is heaven. This is for Sarah," I told my husband. We began to explore it immediately. After that day, we came back for frequent visits to the land that had yet to actually become ours. The auction would be in May. While we waited for that day, I remained alongside Sarah, trying everything to attempt to distract her from her torment. As if to confirm acquisition of the land, days before the auction, my husband received a birthday gift from an artist friend; and it was a landscape painting very similar to the acreage with the phrase "A Distant

Hello, Dr. Wells

Dream" The artist, Greg, knew nothing of the land or our plans to try to buy land. Soon enough Steve would go to the auction.

(5/2005)Hello Dr. Wells,
I just got off the phone from talking to Steve. He and Bret just won the bidding. It was higher than we expected but Bret came alongside during the auction thinking he might use some of the land for a retreat. His involvement allowed enough of a bankroll to finally win the bidding. Sarah slept through the night last night. She woke rested. When she came downstairs this morning she did not do the episodes she usually does upon coming downstairs. She did have a non violent episode about an hour after waking. She had a quiet morning… We took Jana to piano and on the way home Sarah had an episode and was hitting the back of my seat and quite upset. Nothing external was a trigger. It lasted quite a while. She did not hit me.

Now we had a place to endure alongside Sarah, a refuge to accept any outcome. The land and hundred-year-old farmhouse on 80 of 160 acres would cost us roughly 6500 dollars per acre, far above actual market value. After the auction, my brother who works in the trades began to hear gossip of the crazy Californians with money to burn, and how they had paid way too much for some land. He realized they were talking about us—yeah, money to burn. We had a piece of paper that called us owners of this new promise land, and upon reading all the paper work and signing the loan documents, I figured out that we were renting from the bank. From then on, we operated on hope that we might survive the actual payments. Rumors aside, we had bigger preoccupations. Even on the day that we won the bidding, Sarah had little relief. When she was not in torment, she had a joyful spirit. The problem was that it seemed as if we were losing her to complete torment.

(Saturday, 5/21/05)Hello Dr. Wells,
This morning Sarah had some non-violent episodes with the chanting and body movements. For streamlining purposes, "episodes" are when she has repetitive phrases and body

movements. At around noontime she had a more violent episode where she took it out on the back of my seat in the car. At around three p.m., she had an upsetting episode where she was out in the garage doing the chanting and body movements and then came in the house to hit and bite shelving, hurting her teeth. She then beat on Steve and me as we were trying to stop her from causing self-injury. At around five p.m., she had a really bad episode when we arrived at the property we just purchased. She was quite violent and animalistic even bending to the ground to bite the tall grass and then screaming because she had done so. From six to seven p.m. she continued having chanting and body movements becoming violent and hitting and throwing things. We were at a loss as to how to stop injury without becoming part of the conflict. She is more out of control than in control at this time. She is scheduled for next treatment on Monday.

To what had Sarah's mind been given over? When she ate grass as the cattle did, I thought of King Nebuchadnezzar, given over to insanity for a period of years in a place of seclusion. After seven years, he lifted his eyes toward heaven as his sanity had been restored. He then praised and exalted, "…the King of heaven because everything he does is right and all his ways are just." Nebuchadnezzar had his discernment. In Sarah's case we continued to act and to set our will toward God's good purpose, even as complete knowledge about any purpose for her situation was not evident. God was, and would continue to be, the author of her story.

The Saturday episode was just a sign of things to come, because Sunday's was not any better. She had multiple episodes and lots of violence. All the violence resulted from her episodes, since she hated it when they took her over. We involved ourselves in her conflict, since we needed to stop the episodes that caused her outright injury. The doctor felt that Sarah seemed to do better right after the treatments and then regress after a couple of days. A full course of ECT would be necessary, but full course had yet to be determined. Monday was worse than Sunday. Sarah screamed out of the blue, chanted and hit things for almost two hours straight. We drove to her next treatment that day. Grace got us to that appointment. Once there for treatment, they could not get Sarah to stop from the episodes. She was berserk. The doctor in charge for that moment sat in the ECT suite with Sarah and me, while we both waited her out. He found out about our three and a half hour drive back home, and then he called the inpatient unit to secure a room for Sarah. He was not convinced that we would make it home.

ADMISSION NOTES…She presents with worsening aggression since being discharged from the adolescent unit. Since being discharged she has had several episodes in which she bites and hits objects. During these episodes which can last for hours she also hits whoever tries to stop her from hitting the objects. One of these episodes occurred on 5/23/05 in the ECT suite…"
NOTE TO DOCTOR (5/25/05) I wanted to tell you about Sarah's day. I was there when she woke in the morning. She was peaceful but did end up doing the chanting and body movements before she went for ECT. They went on for quite a while. She also did some episodes on the way to ECT and right before taking the mask. I took lunch to Sarah and she did the episodes right after she ate. She continued with them throughout the afternoon, even as we attempted an outing. She did them while in the car, while swimming and while in the tub. The longest period of about 15 minutes where she was not doing her episodes occurred while in the car. Another period of quiet lasted for about ten minutes in the tub. Today I saw her agitated by the episodes upon coming out of them, on a handful of occasions. A few times she had physical outburst toward what was available to put her fist upon (the dash, a book or the hotel bed).

After the occurrence in the ECT suite, I shared some reflections about her body movements and phrases. I needed the doctor to know, even if my synopsis was of little value. I told him that before the fall of 2003 Sarah did not engage in the intense sorts of episodes. The first ones I recognized in 2003 were subtle, with less verbal and occasional short aggression, and she had not been on medication when they first started. Mayo recorded these manifestations when they did EEG in the winter of 2004. Curiously, a first grade report written in 2001 by a specialist, mentioned repetitive phrases and body movements, those happening after screaming and frustration in the classroom; significant enough in duration to be mentioned in the 2001 report, different enough not to be considered as regular stimulatory behavior. I just know that I did not see the verbal phrases combined with body movements in 2001. Could it have been happening at school and not at home? I do recall that Sarah engaged in repetitive phrases when she was under stress, but there were no body movements to accompany the phrases, and they were most evident during her time doing reading and math in resource at school. Her engagement in those phrases seemed entirely different from the echoalia of her earliest years. I remember sending concerns to the developmental specialist about the behavior during the 2002/2003 school year, but I did not convey it well enough to receive meaningful response. I just felt that stress actually mechanized a motor response that Sarah had little control over, and she did not simply engage the behavior for the benefit of escaping her work. At any rate, treatment from Mayo in 2004 resulted in improvement for a short time and she seemed to find relief. We started to notice the newer types of episodes that were at first few in number, and did not seem to result in aggression or bother Sarah. These newer types of episodes amped up, and then she became frequently aggressive in the winter 2005.

I wanted to take Sarah on outings throughout the week, but she began to have a hard enough time that I could not justify bringing her to the hotel where bystanders might be affected. When Steve, who is big and strong, joined us for the weekend, we took her on an outing. She swam a lot—no episodes, no violence, one hundred miles an hour! She move through every activity in high gear, a speed that would not work overall, but was okay considering her present challenges and what we were trying to accomplish. We went to the mall, to the Disney Store, and a bookstore. It had lots of people and lots of noise. She moved fast to accomplish her goal of getting books and an item from the Disney Store, and we ran to keep up with her. We set no limits for shopping or food. We just wanted to make sure she had much success with her outing. With her shopping spree over, we went back to the hotel and she swam for a second time. She began to get into the safety stuff at the pool and we had to set limits. She accepted the limits after sizing us both up. We let her swim until she was ready to be finished. We dropped Sarah off at the unit for the night and continued to hope that our little girl would start to feel better.

We remained hopeful about the next day's outing. We picked her up around noontime, and drove to the hotel where she swam with Jeff and Jana. Sarah rushed to the pool, in high gear again. She seemed agitated at all times, and entirely focused on the internal, in that she could not grant us any attention externally. She fleetingly interacted with us, but her conflicted internal conversations kept overtaking her. She had episodes in the pool and those resulted in screaming, thus interrupting any possibility of her enjoyment in the activity. The interruptions of her episodes became increasingly more frustrating to her. The opportunity for playing and having fun with us seemed to exacerbate the situation. She really wanted to play with us. We offered to take her for a drive, and so she rushed to the room; she refused what would usually be an enjoyable bath, and she dressed herself at manic speed. She then waited for no one else, as she ran to the car while screaming. All I could do was follow her, while the others hurriedly got dressed so that they could come along. Even though the drive was what she wanted to do, she continued engaging in her episodes, her repetitive discontent. I really wondered how we would be able to continue outings to the hotel, or anywhere else, since it involved the public. I kept thinking, stop the world, we need to get off. We took Sarah to the unit for the evening. In the days that followed, I focused on setting things in motion for next steps, per Mayo doctors' instructions.

The team at Mayo seemed worried, since it had been such a long haul. They told me it was time to accept some help, and their advice aligned with what I had already started to feel. I just wanted to be a reliable constant in her never-ending storm, but I started to feel that I was failing her. I met with the local specialty school about placement and that necessitated meeting with the people at the school district as well. I agreed to Sarah's placement in a day program, since keeping her home waiting for sustained improvement did not result in prolonged relief. I was just happy there was programming available that allowed her to come home at night! After setting help in motion, we went to see our Sarah. Once in Rochester we went straight to the unit to pick up Sarah for an outing. She really did not have a good time on the outing and when we brought her back to the unit, she engaged in rudeness towards the professionals there. She slammed her door and wanted to be in the dark of her room. It is hard to explain how that rudeness looked different from all her other difficulties, thus I offer the fact that when the episodes did not completely take her over she had a joyful spirit. When Steve saw her developing a penchant for willful rudeness, and her need to sit in the dark, he asked for her luggage. He then said that we needed to take her home. I looked at Steve and cautioned him, "You realize you will have to be at home with us, right?" He did. I guess the business would have to run a bit lean, until all the new help for Sarah was actually implemented.

(6/6/05)Hello Dr.Wells,
Steve saw Sarah being rude and sitting in the dark at the unit and he decided we should take her home. Heather did get Sarah out of her room in the morning on Sunday and Sarah did some wonderful drawings…did still have some episode. On her outing that same day we also saw too many episodes to count and now she finds it necessary to incorporate others in her them. She also has internal conflict aside of her episodes which is pervasive. She allows for very little limit setting and over very unimportant things. She says "no" to most requests, but complies many times. She was grinding her teeth a lot last night while awake. While she did have Klonopin last night she had many mood swings (anger, crying) that seemed to run a cycle of around ten minutes each. She went through these in between doing some episodes. She was grinding her teeth while crying. She did not fall asleep until after midnight…that was about the time she could be calm enough to do so. If the Klonopin is not helping her sleep, is it having an actual bad effect and keeping her up and unable to sleep? Since she is having the Reminyl two times daily and had a quiet morning yesterday I am assuming it may be okay to keep on board for a while to see if there is any

Hello, Dr. Wells

improvement. The school district agreed to send the expert to our home for evaluation purposes.

The doctor's summary for that most current stay at the unit put most of it in a reliable nutshell. Initially she was combative on admission, and was placed in seclusion temporarily. She was given Thorazine and Ativan to help calm her down. She was admitted for safety, stabilization, and evaluation. She underwent additional ECT treatments for a rare form of periodic catatonia during the hospitalization to bring the total number of ECTs to ten. Unfortunately, the behavior/condition did not improve during the hospitalization. Ativan was used at times to help with behavioral control with questionable benefit. A neurology consult was obtained to further evaluate her repetitive behaviors. The doctor's impression was that Sarah had sleep-state dissociation, with elements of REM sleep becoming super-imposed into wakefulness. The sleep-state dissociation was believed to be the cause of her hallucinatory behavior, and so the doctor recommended that Sarah's environment be well lighted during the day and dark at night. He also recommended Klonopin to help her sleep. Both of these recommendations were enacted. Sarah seemed to become disinhibited following the start of the Klonopin and there was question of whether or not it caused her disinhibition. She was started on a trial of Reminyl. She was only on Reminyl for a couple of days before discharge. Klonopin was of questionable benefit with the possibility of causing disinhibition. Sarah was discharged from the hospital at parent request. Recommendations from the primary treatment team were for Sarah to receive treatment during the days in a structured, supportive environment.

Once back home, we dug in, ready to endure whatever came our way. Sarah continued to have a hard time falling asleep. The Klonopin was a bust, meaning it did not help her sleep. Even with the sleep-state dissociation being an adequate explanation, the medication normally used for such a problem did not help Sarah. I researched the Reminyl and found that if I gave her the dosage in a different way, it might help with the sleep issue; literature offered that it sometimes caused problems in sleep when given in the evening. Reminyl was being used off label. Sarah continued with pervasive episodes, violence toward her surroundings, and sleeplessness. She would not have been manageable in any institution, because no drug calmed her. Day after day, the report remained the same. She tried to involve us in her conflict pervasively, but we refused. Many evenings our house was filled with terrible screams, as Sarah did not recognize us, and had breaks from reality. She had incidental and odd triggers. Things like washing her hair or asking for a hug caused her to get mad at us and call us by a different name. Her memory referred her back to an episode that she had with a professional at the unit; one who had tried to help her with getting showered and brushing her hair. We became that unit professional and Sarah called us by her name. Curiously, nothing bad had happened to trigger that unit event as there had been another incidental trigger responsible for that episode! We became quite able to identify even the most nonsensical of triggers, ones that only made sense to us because we knew Sarah and her life's experiences so well. Most of the triggers that were in place had been instigated by an initial conflict that was caused by either outright hallucinations or internal compulsions; the compulsions in place due to the faulty way she utilizes her memory. It is as if associative thought process is her downfall. Temple Grandin talks about associative thought in *Thinking in Pictures*, but Sarah seemed to take it one step further by thinking in repertoires and then having to re-enact them. Did the fact that we made sense of her psychosis make us crazy? Obviously, I am crazy for Sarah.

∽

Here is an attempt to explain Sarah's susceptibility to triggers (reasons, or causes for some episodes). Sarah's associative thought process does not follow the same rules as a normal person, and so she acts upon her memories differently. In the context of her development of extreme thought disorder, activities that she finds enjoyable have, at some point, been interrupted by her psychosis, her auditory and visual hallucinations, or just a negative everyday experience. The next time she becomes involved in the previously enjoyable activity, her associative thought takes her to the one negative event that transpired during it, the negative event taking precedent over all the pleasant ones that transpired during the very same activity. In addition, her associative thought process may also lend itself to a more pseudo hallucinatory process; in that her mind may recreate the, at first actual, hallucinatory events associated with activities; they may not be as strong as actual hallucinations, but the re creation her mind engages in strongly represents the initial hallucinatory experience. These musing take me to the still unanswerable questions, which came first the hallucination or an every day, consequential stressor? Did stress have anything to do with her psychosis? Was psychosis there simply because it was? Has she always been like this, albeit with less intensity when she was younger?

∾

During the month of June, I found myself frequently informing the doctors of Sarah's episodes. One day, Steve and Jeff suffered her wrath on a drive from the property. It was similar to the rage that Jana and I had suffered previously with her. They actually pulled over to wait her out because she was too quick and insistent in her rage. They could not restrain her without hurting her so they just waited, keeping her from going out on the highway, but allowing her some space. One motorist stopped at the spectacle, not sure what they were witnessing. How could one even explain it? Steve and Jeff did not even bother trying to explain. Overall, she needed space while being kept safe. A little past the middle of June, we began to see signs of incremental and increasing relief for Sarah. Oh, that it could be sustained.

> *(6/22/05)Hello Dr. Wells,*
> *She woke up after a good night's sleep (8:00 p.m. to 6:30 a.m.).*
> *She wanted to hug quite a while. She had her usual episodes and*
> *conflict that were intermittent throughout the morning, but not*
> *ramping up to any degree. At 11:30 a.m. she ramped up (nothing*
> *averse had happened to trigger it) and I gave PRN medication.*
> *At 1:30 p.m. more PRN medication. She requested swimming and*
> *jumping together, and also going for a drive. She was able to accept*
> *some limits without much fuss.*

Ann Dunham

She was quite funny swimming with Jeff's friends, Steve, Jana and me. She got quite a smirk on her face when I had jumped in the pool with my clothes on. She likes Jeff's friends. She chased after Jeff's 6'7" friend and he screamed for help and it was a hoot. She was done with them at about 6:00 p.m. and said exactly this to them, "Go away boys." She spent very creative time with imaginary play in her bedroom creating ingredients for cooking, with paper. Like paper dolls except with the whole food thing going on. She was very happy doing this. One thing she did that struck me...she was holding a paper phone that she made and then she dialed it and said, "Hello, I really need to talk to you." Such a normal sentence and we have been hearing more of this normal talk coming out of her.

Upon the June 22 report, the doctor felt the Reminyl had started to kick in. That was a good thing since Sarah would be starting the day program the following week. She eventually would ride a taxi to school. Look out Mr. Taxi driver. I hoped that those taxi rides might go better than the sometimes problematic drives out to the farm. I made sure that an aide would accompany her on the rides to school.

Chapter 14: To Succeed by Associations

Transition back to school, 2005 (twelve and thirteen years old). While we started to see some improvement, there continued to be trying times. On June 24, we drove to the acreage and along the way; Sarah fell into a spit episode so we told her to stop spitting. She did not spit at us, she just spat repetitively. To her credit, she tried hard not to spit, but it continued and she became agitated, even as we resigned ourselves to overlook the behavior. She then got into a mode of methodically hitting me with great force on my forearm, over and over. Steve told me that it was exactly what happened to him and Jeff on their drive. Steve tried to protect me while driving, in as much as I would not allow Sarah to engage in hitting my arm. She then tried to hit, and then bite me in succession. We pulled off to wait it out and then Sarah beat on Steve and tenaciously grabbed his throat. While she did this, she was beside herself. She tried to talk us into letting her "...hit Mom one more time" and through great agility, she accomplished her goal. When able, we headed home, canceling the trip to the farm. I attempted some as needed usage of medication, never being absolutely sure that it helped. I only hoped that it might contribute to some relief for Sarah. The PRN medications were Risperdal and Ativan; giving one, then the other a couple of hours later seemed to work best.

Sarah woke up with screams on the morning of her first day of school. She had episodes and then calmed down. She rested for a while after that, and eventually headed downstairs to eat some breakfast. Sarah had a few episodes with conflict after eating. Upon calming down from the episodes, she read a note about going to school; it seemed to put her in a good mood, probably because Cortney was going to take her. Sarah became extremely happy about the opportunity to see the young gal who had worked successfully with her before her worsening. I guess it was a good thing that the taxi was not able to start until the following week, because we now had the Cortney effect! She provided an element of positive association for Sarah's transition back into the school environment. Positive associations aside, I still needed to consider the best way to dose the medication. I decided to give Sarah some Risperdal at 9:00 a.m. so that I could follow up with the Ativan a couple of hours later. That type of dosing schedule seemed to have the best outcome in recent days, as giving them at the same time had proven disastrous. Even after the morning dose of Risperdal, Sarah remained in and out of some conflict. She calmed down at around 10:00 a.m. and put on her swimsuit, clothes, shoes, and back pack. She thought it was time to go to school, but when I told her it was not she became a bit peeved even as she accepted the delay. She then jumped on the trampoline with Steve and it was a nice time, since jumping with him sent her flying high into the air! Sarah asked Daddy for "more bounce" quite a few times. When she finished jumping she came in to get ready for school a second time, and then she waited for her ride. Cortney arrived with the added surprise of bringing her mom, previously Sarah's kindergarten teacher. Sarah was so excited. Since Robyn and Cortney had not been around for the more psychotic times, they represented only happy memory associations. The thought associations they provided offered a bigger chance for a successful transition to school. I only hoped that Robyn and Cortney would never see Sarah in torment. I had actually stopped the sessions with Cortney after April suffered the aggression from Sarah. I did not want Sarah to have any negative associations with regard to Cortney, purposefully reserving only safe memories between the two. As they left for school, Cortney asked Sarah for a high five; it did not trigger an episode as it had been. Sarah happily rode to the school and was nice to the aide who met her in the lobby. The first class for school would be lunch period!

Several hours later, when Sarah got off the bus after school, she very calmly said, "No more school for Sarah. It is too loud. It makes Sarah scream and it hurts my ears." I guess her day was filled with screaming in the classroom. She did behave on the bus though. I had to chuckle, because when all was said and done, her main goal seemed to be having some down time in the pool, which she recently wasn't very good at. She purposefully jumped into the pool and seemed happy to be on her own. She remained pleasant for much of the afternoon. For this particular afternoon, day programming seemed the best idea ever!

On the next day, Sarah woke up and we hugged. Sarah talked a lot about not going to school. I told her that the doctor at the school was going to look at her ears. Since her ear had been bugging her previously, she liked the idea of getting to see a doctor at school. She mentioned *not* wanting to swim at school, and bad acoustics was probably be the reason for that (indoor pool). After getting dressed, she insisted that she would *not* be going to school and then she put on her backpack and waited for Cortney, quite willingly. On the drive to school, Cortney asked Sarah if she liked school and yes was the reply. Sarah responded the same when asked about swimming at school. Sarah walked happily over to the aide when she got to school. Later in the day, the teacher told me that Sarah had engaged in much screaming, however she was completing her work. I knew the teachers would not have time to give blow by blow descriptions of Sarah's day so I devised a checklist, hoping they might fill it out so that we could have some indicator if Sarah was improving or not. The school also had a more complicated behavior reporting system.

(6/30/05) Ann's Checklist
Did Sarah?

Cover her ears	*NO*
Hit objects	*NO*
Hit others	*YES*
Scream	*YES (2x)*
Bite herself	*NO*
Bite others	*NO*
Spit	*NO*
Spit upon others	*NO*
Have episodes	*YES (7x)*
Complete her work	*YES*

The Fourth of July holiday approached, and Sarah liked like the idea of having a holiday from school so quickly. We closed on the property on July 1, already having made daily trips to try out the new tractor, affectionately called LeRoy; and to start fixing the farmhouse. As Sarah continued in differing degrees with all her usual suspects, the farm gave her some positive focus. Still, we identified some new triggers that caused episodes—the words "yuck" and "eew" (another form of yuck that sounds like "you"). I am pretty sure these words came about because we ended up going through cow pies while riding the four wheelers. With all the farm adventure and positive focus going on, I felt the need to reinstate better limits with Sarah; there were many ways to deny her requests. Sarah accepted quite a few "nos," but I also used a lot of "maybe later," "soon," or "not right nows." At school I noted that they used "ask me later" as an alternative. They also had an effective method that involved Sarah writing the steps for accepting no, and it seemed to contribute to building that ability in her. At times, I completely ignored some of her request to see how much she really wanted them. Any attempts in using a familiar redirect remained inadvisable, because Sarah would sense that I was manipulating her. In a nutshell, limit setting was doable and obvious redirects were not advisable. She became quite civil about accepting limits, and she did not engage in violence about them, but occasionally she still screamed. Did that mean we were approaching normal teenager territory? (Ha)

Over the holiday weekend in July, she asked me to laminate a cell phone that she had drawn, and I cut out; because I was not sure about letting her have scissors yet. She used her laminated cell phone for talking to her more imaginary crowd, and she even kept it in her shorts pocket like her brother Jeff did with his. While Jeff's phone was real, Sarah understood that hers was not. I asked her to call her Daddy with her phone and she looked at me as if I had lost my mind. She liked the whole laminating thing so much that she asked me to laminate her recently drawn picture of a gun. I think she wanted that because the boys used paint ball guns out at the farm recently. Later, she actually used her laminated gun when I had set a limit about something, and I was just glad it did not have paint ball pellets. While she used her cell phone throughout the day, she only used the gun once. I became excited because Sarah was starting to engage in creative activities again, but the icing on the cake was her wonderful use of language. I sent a report to the doctors about her increasing language improvement. I explained that Sarah jumped in the pool with her clothes on and subsequently started to take her shorts off in the water. I asked Sarah not to take her shorts off and told her that it would be better to go in and get her swimsuit. She responded by putting her shorts back on and telling me, "No Mom, that's okay," in such a natural way. It was as if she had been talking all her life. I was also encouraged because she was at no point naked in the back yard, which had happened with some regularity when Sarah had been doing worse just days ago.

With the short break over and school back in session, Sarah immediately talked about not going. She went to school in spite of her protests, and had many school days like the first; and that was actually encouraging. Nevertheless, there continued to be peaks and valleys that had no particular pattern that could identify cause.

7/11/05 Checklist
Did Sarah?

Cover her ears	*NO*
Hit objects	*NO*
Hit others	*YES (15x)*
Scream	*YES (50x)*
Bite herself	*NO*
Bite others	*Attempt (4x)*
Spit	*YES (on staff 8x)*
Have episodes	*YES (25x)*
Other	*Kick (5x) and throw scooter at staff (1x)*

Through July, Sarah continued with her challenges. The violent behaviors at school incrementally decreased to the point of flat lining in August. That being said, the only behaviors they needed to track for their purposes were to do with actual violence and non-compliance. The checklist I devised had stopped coming home so I could never be sure that the episodes, that were repetitive and more catatonic in nature, had completely extinguished. I really needed to know if she was having her repetitive episodes, and I needed to know the frequency. I started to notice Sarah re-enacting self-abusive behaviors in a sort of slow motion, and I figured it might be stuff she witnessed at school. I frequently redirected her from those behaviors. I did not want her to become so good at them that she did them at regular speed. She also picked up on the foul language in which some of her classmates engaged. When she first displayed the new behaviors they did not appear extreme in nature, nor did they precipitated anything. She did slow enactments of banging her head with her fist, scratching herself, and sometimes she cursed; but it seemed entirely for novelty sake. When I mentioned the behaviors to one of her teachers, she confirmed that Sarah was imitating what went on in the classroom. For crying out loud, why did Sarah have to be so good at imitating? I just hoped that she would not include her newly learned behaviors in any future episodes, should they once again return in force during any worsening psychosis. During this time of improvement, we had a planning meeting to discuss lengthening Sarah's school day. All the teachers wanted to lengthen the school day in the behavior room before transitioning Sarah to public school again. I agreed with that concept, but worried that the seasonal component might rear its ugly head when September came again.

For many at the meeting it was all about excellent programming and success that it seemed to provide, but I had seen the trap that would snare with regard to the seasonal challenge. The ebb and flow to Sarah's wellness and performance was very evident throughout the years.

> *(8/4/05)Hello Dr. Wells,*
> *I do not know how to articulate to them that Sarah only bites and spits when she is troubled with worsening psychosis...The hitting was always associated with her mostly psychotic episodes, and before she entered the 4th grade, she had not hit people. I am happy she is doing well. I do not think they understand the big picture about Sarah. I fear that they think she is doing well, but only because of their structure and behavioral supports. When Sarah got worse during her 4th grade year, she had the best structure and routine that could be given (at home and school). We tried to keep her in that structure and it did not help her to get better. We backed*

off from teaching and tried meds and she began to recover to some degree so that we could reintroduce structure. There is an ebb and flow to her problem that has nothing to do with her environment, or the things transpiring in it.

There was a three-week break shortly after the planning meeting. Toward the end of the break, we had a campout at the farm—family, friends, and a good time. When we were out in the cool of the evening, some began to toss a football. Sarah became engaged in the activity and all of a sudden said, "Daddy, I am so full of happiness." Later when she was asleep, we all marveled at her expression of satisfaction. Her happiness seemed to extend to the resumption of school in the first week of September.

Chapter 15: To Succumb by Seasons

(11/8/05)Hello Dr. Wells,
We have seen the emergence of the repetitive phrases and body movements at home. I just wanted to let you know. I suspect they have begun again at school, as the behavior cards have increased. I know she has been doing it on the bus on occasion. Screaming is part of one of the repetitive episodes she does. A short burst of screaming with some phrases. Thanking a doctor is part of another one. When she comes out of the episode, she seems fine and resumes whatever she was previously engaged in. We have noted that the words "good" and "better" seem to trigger the episodes. Previous word triggers last year were "hurry" and "there you are." We really like to limit the verbal load we are giving her when this is happening. I suspect she will become more frustrated the more invasive the episodes become, and will begin to become violent, towards mostly objects, and sometimes people who are interrupting her during them. That is the pattern we have seen the past three winters. The potty mouth stuff has not worsened, but is still evident. Not towards us, but during her acting out of the events that she experiences at school. I have tricked Sarah into replacing the actual cuss words with "forget you" and "poser." At least it allows for some expression without actual foul language, a little less inappropriate. As long as she is exposed to other kids using such language, she will continue to do it due to her love for imitation.

We just kept trying, 2005 and 2006 (twelve and thirteen years old). Behavior cards coming from the school dramatically increased. The episodes emerged at school and at home. They ebbed and they flowed seeming to do whatever they wanted, whenever they wanted. They seemed like a meditative state that took over Sarah. They were almost always distressing and upsetting to her. Her will seemed to want to control the problem, but will was not enough. She definitely tried fighting the onset of them, but was hopeless to do battle and stop them. The school's behavior cards indicated where, when, and possibilities of why the behaviors occurred. However, understanding about what the episodes represented in Sarah's case was not immediately complete, not until the school's experts observed. Once she fell into the episodes, triggers hardly mattered. It did not matter if someone asked her to do something before the event, and it did not matter if someone provoked her. Any observable reason was of little consequence, since there remained many more unidentifiable reasons. Place, time, extraordinary events, incidental happenings, and words all became a trigger. Her associative thought process made it all bad! How could we stop everything from being a trigger? To remove all triggers would mean the padded room with nothing and nobody in it.

Musings about Sarah's catatonic type episodes and if they were calculated: The idea that she used the episodes as a form of manipulation or attention seeking needed challenging. Throughout the worse times, I did my own experimentations to see if what was outwardly occurring made a difference in Sarah's episodes. Early on, I engaged in the method of ignore and re-direct for much longer than I should have, so I will not waste time explaining about that. Throughout one troubling period, I purposefully allowed all things for which she asked. Luckily, she did not request the very expensive or impossible things. While affecting our savings, it proved worth doing. What I discovered over several months, was the fact that it did not matter if she attained all that she desired. The episodes continued in full force even as her wants realized ongoing fulfillment. She actually ran out of things to want, which could actually represent a completely new scenario in this musing. Additionally, I also watched her episodes continue when no teaching had transpired, and no expectations had been placed upon her. In all my curiosities, I have come to know that there are mostly nonsensical reasons for the catatonic type episodes that result in outbursts. Wants, needs, or even expectations placed upon her have little to do with them, especially once they become pervasive.

༒

By December, the school eventually reported duration, and if the episodes occurred before the outburst. At first, if she was engaged in an episode and did not comply with a directive, they assumed she did the behavior and the resulting outburst because of their request, instead of recognizing that the episode started before their request. Everyone figured out that most of her episodes had nothing to do with their requests, demands, or expectations. At school, intervention against the episodes was rarely successful.

Also in December, the bus aides who rode home with Sarah became quite concerned because she was spacing out and not responsive. Sarah's more intoxicated nature seemed to have come back; during these particular days, there was an instance when I rescued her from the back yard pool that had frozen over. She was supposed to be going downstairs to wait for the bus, and then I heard her scream, quickly finding that she had walked upon on the pool ice. I found her waist deep in the freezing water. I jumped in with her and then we utilized a ladder for climbing out of the pool; had it not been there we would have both been frost bitten. The ladder was within reach of the area that Sarah was stuck in, so with much force and breaking of the ice I was able to move the ladder so that we could get out. Later that day Sarah told her dad, "The ice. It broke. Help. Help. And Mommy saved my life!" On a more positive note, Sarah had a great birthday party in December; it actually brought her father to tears.

(12/11/05) Hello Dr. Wells,
Her party was a success. Sarah was thrilled. She picked the people who went. Chuck E. Cheese came out to do Sarah's birthday dance and we all joined in. Everyone was just thrilled with how she stayed with the dancing the whole time, even with the encore. She even did the waltz with Chuck E. Cheese. As she did the dancing, with everyone joining in she was so happy, it seemed such a normal

happy time. As her dad took pictures, he just broke down crying because it so richly blessed him. All total she was at the party for one and a half hours. Towards the end, we saw a rapid increase in the behaviors and knew it was time to leave and end on a good note.

During this time, Sarah had started to have problems with throwing up. We kept an eye on her at home and the school began keeping an eye on things there. Initially we thought she had the flu, but as the problem persisted, we all realized the vomiting was not flu related. We wondered if it was due to too much fluid intake. Sarah started to drool quite a bit about this time. She had some sensations that would cause her to scream and hold her head. I did not know if it was due to what she was feeling in her head, or if she was hearing things that were upsetting to her. She did some weird breathing that she accompanied with head movements and swallowing. She even positioned her entire body in a certain way, sometimes becoming agitated, almost to the point of physically acting out. It had become quite difficult at school.

School personnel were taken aback by her winter worsening. They had a discrete trial in mind for Sarah's insistence that doors remain shut, and while that might have addressed one of her problems, I needed to know what the team thought was about her more schizophrenic tendencies. I asked what the interventions might be when Sarah was clearly hallucinating. I did not get an answer, and that made me wonder how much consideration the more troubling psychosis received. Perhaps, considerations of functionality in the classroom with regard to overt psychosis, was not the purpose of the behavior room. Admittedly, finding medications or treatments that gave sustained relief of schizophrenic symptoms remained the role of her doctors. It seemed the most tangible regret at this time remained that of ignoring hindsight. A look at many winters of medical records answered the worsening question. A look at her educational records pointed a trend out as well. It was all in the documented history. While it always remains important to be positive and forward thinking with regard to helping people like my daughter, it also remains beneficial to know the history so that one is not blindsided. My thought is that the school suffered great disappointment at Sarah's worsening, because she represented fulfilled hope to them. I guess they did not know that they still represented hope fulfilled for our entire family because they endured through good times and the worst times, alongside Sarah.

Because of the worsening, the school nurse called with questions about medication and I informed her that nothing had been changed. Together we reviewed Sarah's medical records and what she had on file did not verify hallucinations, even though I gave permission for them to access records. I had also made many attempts to verbally inform them, since before Sarah started school. Even without the records, the nurse felt that Sarah hallucinated. We talked about the lack of documentation, and she assured me that she would get the complete record. As we talked a bit further, the nurse had an "Aha!" moment. Her eyes widened as she found out why I had not used their school doctor. The school had been somewhat troubled because they thought I did not want their highly respected doctor, whom they had recommended in the first planning meeting. I told the nurse that I called their doctor and his office refused to make an appointment, even interrupting me while I tried to explain that Sarah was in the day program, under his auspice. I informed the school social worker on Sarah's team about it when it happened, and our agreement was that the school could pursue it as an issue if they wanted him for internal purposes. During very difficult times with Sarah, I was not about to argue with anyone about the need to help. Sarah already had some excellent doctors anyway.

The school continued to track behaviors in their customary way, but they had also started to journal Sarah's episodes. December, and then January passed. Sarah's throwing up increased and she indicated issues of pain in her head. The episodes took her over at school, and at home.

Hello, Dr. Wells

...Sarah has been stuck in her episodes and doing them all through the night. Here are the behavior cards from Friday.

Date: 1/27/06
Time: 9:35 a.m.
Location: Library
What happened before? Another child walked by.
Behavior: Kicking
Duration: 1x

Time: 11:40 a.m.
Location: Class
What happened before? Was doing worksheets.
Behavior: Screaming
Duration: 30 minutes

Time: 12:20 p.m.
Location: Dining Room
What happened before? Eating lunch.
Behavior: Screaming, hitting, kicking wall
Duration: 30 minutes, 10x, 8x

Time: 2:15 p.m.
Location: Class
What happened before? Asked to do something.
Behavior: Screaming
Duration: Unknown

Time: 1:55 p.m.
Location: Class
What happened before? Asked to do something.
Behavior: Screaming, hitting, kicking
Duration: 2 minutes, 2x, 1x

I wanted to mention that the worksheets are independent work, so when she screamed there was no one with her, and she was just at her table doing work. Nobody provoked it. Also at lunch, I think she was probably doing the episodes and could not stop...Especially if there was *food in front of her that she wanted to eat. When she got off the bus, she walked straight in the house and began the episodes. It took a while for her to stop and come willingly to the car for a drive to the farm. I had food waiting in the car but she did not get to it. She was doing the episodes for the entire forty-minute drive to the farm. She cried during that time, asking if we could make the french fries hot at the farm. At the farm, she continued the episodes for about a half hour more. She then came in and watched Jana and I bake a cake. She continued with the episodes only stopping for a piece of cake that was sitting in front of her, and to have a bath. I gave her Ativan hoping it would help her sleep or at least calm the episodes. She did not sleep and was into the episodes screaming for help. I tried to help but could not. By about 3 a.m. she allowed me to rub her head and cradle it. Since she was so tired, she fell asleep with her head in my arms. She stayed asleep maybe 30 minutes.*

Saturday she continued with the episodes and it interfered with her normal farm routine. Tried to get her mind going in a different direction by taking her on the quad...she threw up so she had a bath instead. She was not doing her episodes for quite a while after she threw up. She did eventually start again. Sarah was able to eat some soup and crackers before having her meds. She had some Ativan about an hour after her regular meds and went to bed. She seemed to fall asleep but I did hear the breathing episodes and she came to check on me one time. I tucked her back in and then I believe she slept for the night.

On Sunday, Sarah was up at 7am screaming and asking for help because she could not stop her episodes. I would try to comfort her. She is just more into her episodes than with us. She is becoming angry because she has a hard time stopping it. She hits herself, and bites herself, and sometimes hits and kicks her surroundings.

Since the doctors at Mayo remained informed about Sarah, they did not hesitate to offer admitting her when worsening occurred. She was placed on the waiting list for a stay at the unit, mostly due to concern about her throwing up. During the very last days in January, we took Sarah to the local ER since we were not sure how long it would take to get her admitted to the unit. We felt overwhelming concerned about the persistent vomiting and the possibility of some digestive issue. The ER did an x-ray of her intestinal track, and some blood tests, and no problems were indicated. The ER doctor watched some of the episodes and he became inquisitive. He asked if she had any head trauma recently, and I responded that she might have, since there had been one head-banging incident reported during the previous week at school. He decided to do a CT of her head. That scan indicated a "…small lacunar infarct in the right basil ganglia" and it was compared to a February 2003 scan of Sarah that was normal.

We actually received a call from Mayo as we left the ER, much to the relief of the ER doctor. Mayo told us that a room was available, and we wasted no time in getting there. Once there, the doctors started diagnostics on Sarah's gut issues. Her esophagus had no damage and her tummy looked good, actually proving the absence of ruminating. If she had been making herself throw up, there would be damage to her esophagus. Curiously, she still had food in her belly even though she had not eaten during the previous 16 hours. The doctors wanted to perform another test to identify blockage that might be occurring. That test ruled out blockage and even confirmed that Sarah's pyloris was as it should be. They reviewed the CT from the ER and wanted to perform their own MRI. After reviewing their scans, they said the particular type of spot that was indicated is linked to a certain type of catatonia. They also confirmed stroke.

With the issue of catatonia being entertained again, an Ativan challenge was considered to be appropriate. For some who have exhibited catatonia, this type of intervention has alleviated symptoms. On the day that the challenge began for Sarah, the nurse and I talked. She told me how they would administer the medication. I had already read that the best way to administer such a challenge was with an IV, but the doctors opted for oral administration. I asked the nurse if Sarah's difference in metabolizing might be a factor. Even though metabolizing had been a factor in her past, the doctors did not consider it important for this endeavor. The nurse started the challenge and Sarah seemed to be episode free for two hours. After that, even as the medication was continued, the episodes returned.

Unfortunately, the doctors gave Sarah sinus medicine along with the second Ativan dose. I wondered if that made the challenge moot for Sarah, since Sudafed and Benedryl had already proven to be disinhibiting to her. The doctors did not agree with my assumptions and felt the challenge ineffective, thus they ordered its discontinuation.

I did wonder how the Ativan could help, considering how long the episodes had been a part of Sarah. Perhaps longer than any of us knew, considering the way they evolved and changed over the years. The episodes might have always been with her to some underlying degree, only manifesting with a more obvious certainty when she had her worsening. The possibility of drug induced malignant catatonia had been ruled out after blood tests. Did malignant catatonia come about on its own with her? The doctors wanted to try ECT again. I wondered about that too. While it may help individuals who have recently fallen under the spell of the differing types of catatonia, how would it help a person who may have had it her entire life in differing degrees? This is just me, wondering if ECT only worked on a brain that has some normal to fall back upon. Sarah may have been permanently hard wired with the dispositions to catatonia. I prayed about it, and left it to God and the doctors. Whenever ECT was considered, protocol necessitated the approval from a certain number of doctors. The last doctor to be called in discussed Sarah's case with me, and he ultimately felt that ECT was not indicated as purposeful for her situation. All that was left to do was to go home. We went home with an assurance that the doctors could do nothing else to help Sarah. We just kept trying to help her. She resumed her attendance at school. The month of April was the worst.

Date: 4/24/06

Time: 9–9:30 a.m.
Location: Class
Behavior: Laughing at self (5x), non compliance (25min), throw Item (3x), property destruction, spitting (4x), threat (3x), hitting attempt and actual (20x), kicking (3x), deep breath/nodding head (15x), talk to self (8x), push staff (12x), clawing at table (12x)

Hello, Dr. Wells

Time: 9:30–10 a.m.
Location: Class
Behavior: Spitting (1x), threat (8x), hitting actual and attempted
(1x), kicking actual and attempted (3x), deep breath/nodding head
(36x), talking to self (27x), pushing staff (12x)

Time: 10:30 a.m.
Location: Class
Behavior: Property dest. (1min), nodding head/deep breathing (30x),
talking to self (33x)

Time: 11:00–11:30 a.m.
Location: Lunch
Behavior: Talking to self (6x), spitting (20x), swearing (15x), threat
(2x), hitting actual and attempted (7x), throw object (4x), grabbing
staff (2x), nodding head/deep breath (22x)

Time: 11:30–12 noon
Location: Lunch
Behavior: Spitting (2x)

Time: 12:20 p.m.
Location: Pool
Behavior: Spitting (10x), kicking (4x)

Time: 1:15 p.m.
Location: Class
Behavior: Property dest. (7x), spitting (11x), swearing (8x), hitting
actual (5x), biting self (3x), nodding head/deep breathing (16x),
talking to self (16x), self abuse (6x)

Time: 1:30 p.m.
Location: Class
Behavior: Spitting (4x), threat (8x), kicking (1x), biting (1x), throw
object (1x), repetitive behavior (30min), talking to self (30min), self
abuse (2x)

Ann Dunham

Time: 2:00 p.m.
Location: Gym
Behavior: Spitting (20x), threat (15x), hitting (1x), kicking wall (1x), repetitive behavior (30min), talking to self (30min)

Time: 2:30 p.m.
Location: Class
Behavior: Self abuse (4x), talking to self (30min), repetitive behavior (30min)

Time: 3:05 p.m.
Location: Class
Behavior: Threat (10x), throw object (1x), repetitive behavior (20min), pretend bite (7x)

Some other manifestations that were recorded in the days that immediately followed were: pushing invisible items off her table, hand to groin, biting imaginary objects off the wall, kicking invisible items, hitting wall, pulling pants way up, biting table, sticking out tongue, hitting tree, and many other activities with "invisible" items. The behaviors actually became more intense on March 26. I then informed the Mayo doctors that things were as hard as they could possibly get, she was just full blown psychotic. I did not feel comfortable sending Sarah to school. I had actually been told to come and get her from school on some days. The school nurse agreed that Sarah would not even be able to stay under their residential care, because nothing was available to control her symptoms. That and nothing seemed to allow Sarah sleep. We tried local treatment, because a doctor at Mayo said he had no new ideas for treating Sarah and no beds were available. Trileptal was tried during initiations of local treatment, but it showed no positive effect and Sarah soon ended up in the local inpatient unit. During this time, we lost Uncle Mark to very tragic circumstance; he was one who had gone before Sarah in living with issues of psychosis. He really understood what she dealt with.

☙

Chapter 16: Grace for Sarah

(5/10/06) Sarah has been in the unit here for about a week. While they have clearly seen her hallucinate, they send mixed signals about it. One minute saying it is beyond behavioral and the next saying that she knows what she is doing is wrong and we need to set limits. What she needs is reassurance in order that she may calm down at some point. There are a couple of nurses that have identified that Sarah is just screaming for help. They are the ones who have been in the field for a long time. I am supposed to sit down with the doctors and educational people tomorrow. Don't really know how that will go. They started giving Sarah Lithium yesterday, along with Seroquel.

Grace is the foundation, 2006 and 2007 (thirteen and fourteen years old). During this time, one of her longer known doctors thoughtfully offered a key point about Sarah's baseline function; it differed greatly from what she displayed in her worse times. It would be hard for professionals to appreciate that such differences in functionality could exist, if they had not seen her over time. The local doctors tried to get to know Sarah. One doctor's focus was on Sarah's fixation and utilization of cartoon content (ruminating), during hallucinations and episodes—while normal people utilize all that they see and hear when they fall into psychosis, Sarah's utilization of her preoccupations seemed to negate the possibility that she was hallucinating. The doctor felt that we needed to figure out why Sarah was ruminating and then how to fix it. Catatonia had previously been the culprit, the seemingly plausible explanation for the manifestations that occurred with and without triggers. It seemed to me that Sarah's catatonia represented a kind of seasonal affect disorder that created the weirdest "depression." The newest doctors talked back and forth about Sarah not fitting the autism label, but also not fitting anywhere else. My hindsight was of little value, but I did ask them when I could take Sarah on an outing.

(5/11/06) We took Sarah on an outing today. We left the unit at 1:45 p.m. with Sarah saying, "So long suckers." Sarah ate McDonald's in the truck while we drove to the farm. She did engage in repetitive hitting of the truck window and repetitive screaming about Zach. She also screamed a high-pitched scream that seemed to be a result of internal stimuli, and had no repetitive nature to it. We got to the farm at about 2:30 p.m. and Sarah got out of the truck and did her repetitive breathing and head nodding. Steve and I attempted to encourage her to get her flannel and shoes on so that we could go for a ride on the quad. She aggressed towards us because she was dealing with her episodes and we had tried to redirect her. She eventually got on the quad but then aggressed and got off to do more episodes. She clawed at the ground, swiped her arm and bit something imaginary with great force. We drove away from her for less than a minute and then drove back to where she was. She got on the quad. She then rode happily for about thirty minutes. She went in the farmhouse to watch a movie and then destroyed the VHS tape. When it was time to go I told her so and she became angry and aggressive toward me, in that she shoved me while holding both my arms. She wanted to stay at the farm and spend the night. I told her she had to go back to the unit. She yelled for the police. I told her that I would take myself to the police after I took her to the unit. That seemed to satisfy her and so she got in the truck to go back. As we drove she stated she doesn't like me anymore and wants a new mom. She reminded me about the police. As we got very close to the unit she saw a police car and said, "There you are!" That was our outing.

Sarah continued on Seroquel and Lithium. They also started her on Clonidine. Since her initial worsening had coincided with starting menses, they started her on Depo Provera. At the unit, they resorted to giving her Chloral Hydrate for sleep at night, since the other medications that normally sedate had little effect on her. The next day's outing had some good and some bad. The dose of Seroquel had been titrated up that day. Sarah was able to have some fun in between her troubles. The end result of the outing was that Steve and Jeff had to carry Sarah into the unit. She went directly to the time out room. After a nursed reasoned with her in the time out room, she verbally complied that she should not *hit*. Then when she left the time out room, she came after me to *bite* my arm. She went back to the seclusion room, and I wrote a report for the doctors. I was really sad. I needed to toughen up for Sarah. The day after, I brought a couple things to the unit for Sarah and told staff to let her know that she could not have an outing because she was too mean. I asked them to tell Sarah I would see her tomorrow.

The plan the doctors set in motion was to have Sarah go to a couple of half-days of school during the following week, to see if the teachers felt there was any improvement. Per usual Sarah had captivated the professionals at the unit in spite of her challenges, causing them to decide that she was better. That they thought her better was at first mind boggling to me, but then I referred my thoughts to the previous caution from Sarah's longer known doctor about her baseline. What I thought about my daughter held very little weight for the local doctors, and so the teacher's reports would have to say it all. At least the teachers knew Sarah's baseline. I just kept taking her on outings as much as was appropriate. Sarah did not really get any better as they titrated up on the Seroquel, and her sleep continued to be interrupted. In the days that followed, I transported Sarah to school. Those first mornings back Sarah was seemingly more subdued, but upon the extension of the school day, all the usual problems returned. The school's behavior cards gave record per half hour, from beginning to end of the school day.

Date: 5/22/06

Time: 9:00–9:30 a.m.
Behaviors: Repetitive episodes, slapping down beside her, holding breath, facial grimace, self talk, self injury.

Hello, Dr. Wells

Time: 9:30–10:00 a.m.
Behaviors: Swipe at air, plug ears, self talk, property destruction, spitting, running away, verbal aggression, hitting, grabbing staff.

Time: 10:00 a.m.
Behaviors: Self talk, grab staff, hitting wall, pulling pants up, screaming, spitting, swearing, aggression, scratching, hitting, biting, throwing objects.

Time: 10:30–11:00 a.m.
Behaviors: Grabbing air, kicking air, hit wall, non compliance, throwing things, plug ears, grabbing staff, property destruction, screaming, aggression, hitting.

Time: 11:00–11:30 a.m.
Behaviors: Pull up pants, wave hands in face, self talk, aggression. During lunch.

Time: 11:30 a.m.–12:00 p.m.
Behaviors: Spitting, kicking, self talk. On playground.

Time: 12:00–12:30 p.m.
Behaviors: Swiped at air, self talk, pull up pants, grabbing staff, screaming, spitting, swearing hitting floor, kicking wall, throwing objects. During swimming.

Time: 1:00–1:30 p.m.
Behaviors: Grab staff, non compliance, pull up pants, screaming, running away, hitting, self talk, licking item.

Time: 1:30 p.m.
Behavior: Pull up pants, hitting chair, swipe at air, hitting table, self talk, nodding head, screaming. Around 2:00 p.m., she began self injury again and the school is concerned about damage. They are considering some sort of restraint, which they usually don't want to do.

Ann Dunham

The school felt Sarah was not better. We were outright being told that she needed to be placed somewhere. The medications did not help, and a plan for adjustment of the medications was not in place. The one local doctor who needed to lead the efforts seemed done in his endeavors, or at least in a harmful holding pattern.

(5/24/06)Hello Dr.Wells,
The doctor's staff put off letting me know what the lithium levels were since yesterday. They even told me they did not have the results. I called the lab today to see if there was a problem and that is when I found out that the results were sent to the doctor yesterday. Today, the doctor's staff told me they did not have the results. After I called the lab, his staff admitted to having the results but they didn't want to give them to me. I just wanted to know because Sarah is doing so poorly and I am still hoping higher levels of lithium may help. The doctor does not want to increase lithium. His staff resents the time and energy Sarah requires. I sense this because they reminded me that he has other patients to see. What a schmuck am I?

The local consensus was that Sarah was a lost cause. They told me that no further medication adjustments needed to happen, and they seemed to hold little interest in my thoughts about her wellness. Since a cause is never over until someone fails to lead it, I made a request for help to Dr. Wells on the morning of March 25. I told him that Sarah was having episodes, and she was injuring herself through one of the behaviors. She started to throw chairs in the kitchen. She then grabbed a knife out of the kitchen, in order to stab holes in a certain area of the hall, ripping at the sheetrock as well. I took the knife and put it back and she tried to get it. I would not let her and so she started to attack me. She needed the knife to get rid of the wall. We learned that whatever the focus of a repetitive behavior was, in this case hitting or spitting at a certain area of a wall, she must get rid of it. That area of the wall offended her as a trigger and so she placed the blame there. I had seen the same with regard to movies that had become triggers. She pulled them out of the VHS player and ripped the tape out of the case. I was still making sense of the craziness. After all, when my brother had done some remodeling in our house, Sarah would watch as he cut into sheetrock, renovating to get rid of some offensive areas!

By the afternoon of March 25, my husband and I dropped a very combative Sarah off at the Mayo unit. A portion of the drive felt like hell on wheels, since Sarah ripped the car seats and tore Steve's shirt completely off him. I ended up needing to drive, because for this particular time, Steve endured the full brunt of her discontent. Upon our arrival to the unit, we became joyful because we made it in one piece; Sarah actually took herself to the seclusion room. So began another stay at the unit. Generose represented another place of refuge, because it allowed more time for mercy and grace. Sarah's stay with them provided another chance to continue the cause to fruition. A significant part of her journey resided within this place and alongside the people in it. The cause, in and of itself, was grace. The Mayo unit and many who worked there began to represent so much. After seeing Sarah situated at the unit, I took my husband home. I returned to be with her the next morning. Once back at Mayo I contacted Dr. Wells to thank him, and to mention some concerns about the continued use of Seroquel. I also let him know about the previous doctor's refusal to up the Lithium dose so that Sarah would be at a therapeutic level. He replied.

(5/26/06) …She started to respond quickly to the Thorazine. This is not a long term medicine, but I want quick improvement so that we can then look at longer term strategies. I am very glad she is here. I have never seen her doing as poorly as she was yesterday or early this morning. I felt terribly for her. She was really frightened.

ᏆᎧ

Even with all her difficulties, I asked the doctors about trying an outing after a couple of days, a short one. I explained that I had talked to the person at the hotel about Sarah and her difficulties and I gave assurance that Sarah would swim when it was not busy. The gal said not to worry because she used to work with people like Sarah. The doctors approved the outing and Sarah enjoyed it. I continued to do

Ann Dunham

the outings while the doctors adjusted the Lithium medication; and that adjustment took some time. Waiting for this newest medication adjustment felt a whole lot better than the waiting to do nothing. The newest team of Mayo doctors asked about Sarah. Her hallucinations challenged them. They asked me to explain my thoughts about Sarah's use of words and phrases from cartoons. They wondered if the hallucinations were more about Sarah ruminating content and less about hallucinating. Their curiosity seemed like a really weird case of déjà vu for me, but the important difference between their thoughts and the local doctors' thoughts was that I was offered to engage in some input. I tried to explain it to the doctors, but I got all tongue-tied. I am terrible at conveying things verbally and so I wrote the doctor.

(5/30/06)Hello Dr. Wells,

I wanted to clarify about the question I was asked today. I do not know if this answers the question better. I was asked about the different words Sarah uses being related to cartoons. This was the same interest that one of the local doctors had. They had been curious if Sarah was just echoing in delayed fashion for some reason, or ruminating. I would have to agree that she has done this in the past with the different content of animated cartoons or movies that she has watched throughout the years.

In the context of how she is doing it now, it is not scripted in a way that makes it relate to the content of the cartoons and movies in which she previously had interest. It is now used in a fashion that makes absolutely no sense, in relation to how she had previously felt about the characters or content of those differing media. Good has become bad and bad has become good. Lots of conflict where there was none before.

I remember one local doctor pointing out how schizophrenic hallucinations have to relate to things that are going on in society at the time. Like my Great Uncle Pat who was schizophrenic. He would think that loud speakers were going off in the city when they were not. He would think that the secret service was listening in on him at all times; he had issues with electronics of that time and

207

may have heard voices from them. He had been a courier for the secret service and had actually suffered head injury during one of his assignments. At any rate, the local doctor was trying to make the point that Sarah could not be hallucinating but rather was delusional. His point was lost on me because cartoons have been Sarah's world, her society, for all of her life. She has not paid close attention to the paradigms of our day.

Simply put, there are times that you can see that she is void of any control or reason and is out of her mind with hallucinations. We just want her to get the help she needs. We also know that we see a progression that starts from the repetitive behaviors, to catatonia like, and then increases in intensity and duration from fall toward winter. In the winter, she begins to have trouble with sleeping and we begin to see hallucinations accompanied with aggression. You also know that she begins to do quite well starting June/July. Then the repetitive stuff is not present for a while until the progression once again begins.

Sometimes I became so frustrated about the questions with regard to Sarah's hallucinations. I did not want her to have them; I hated them. Her Uncle Mark suffered from them for many years before his passing on this very same year. He described what they were like and how they fooled him, since he believed them to be real. It took a while for him to realize the tricks his mind played on him. He had both visual and auditory hallucinations, caused from bruising on the brain from a motorcycle accident. He told me about the first time the visual hallucination came, and how it seemed absolutely real to him. He told me about the auditory ones, and how he constantly battled them. For him, the hallucinations reserved their very own place in a particular room or setting—yes, the room and settings as the triggers. New places gave relief for a short while, until the hallucinations decided to relocate with him. When Mark told me these things, I easily believed him because I had already seen much of what he described while discerning Sarah's issues. I had also read about one schizophrenic who recovered after adolescence. She said that her thoughts became stronger, becoming actual voices in her head and eventually the visual hallucinations accompanied the auditory ones. It is scary to think that hallucinating has such an ordered process, and it makes me grateful for every day that I am sane.

We kept trying the outings. Sarah did not level out as much as the doctors would have liked, but everyone just kept trying. The doctor's main focus continued to be that of getting Sarah's lithium level where it needed to be. During one meeting, he posed a question to me about which medication through the years seemed to give any kind of lasting benefit. I stuttered, but when all was said and done, it seemed to be Risperdal. I had a love hate relationship with it because of the weight gain, but it really did lessen the aggression and intensity of outbursts. The Paxil, Abilify, Buspar, Cogentin, Luvox, Strattera, Depakote, Geodon, Klonapin, Reminyl, Clonidine, Trileptal, and Seroquel trials had seemed to either make her worse, or not sustainably better. Forgive me if I have forgotten any of the tried medications! Professionals at the unit experimented with the Risperdal dosage while they observed Sarah, and they were quite diligent throughout the process. It would take time for Lithium to be of benefit and it would take time for Sarah's winter to go away. At least she might sleep while we waited for her to get better, since the doctors identified a combination of two different sleep aids that actually caused Sarah to sleep well. Those were Lunesta and Rozerem. She went for days on end without sleep at times, and that definitely did not help her condition. When she left the unit on June 7, on that first night back home, we ALL rested; and that had not happened for a long time. I did not know how things would go overall, but the whole being able to sleep thing felt exhilarating and liberating.

After a good nights sleep, Sarah got into a little redecorating. Essentially, she wanted to empty the house of all triggers, which was actually almost everything she used to play with. A new phrase she liked to use was, "Get rid of it" and it did seem important to remove unnecessary stimulation, in order for Sarah's mind to have less occupation by her crowd of associations. Anti-decorating became the newest trend in our home. Gone was her large Mickey Mouse, her many movies with all their differing themes, her many toys, and other long time familiar things. Doing this served Sarah well because it seemed to result in significantly less anxiety for her, making our home a place for her mind to rest. It was not that the items were bad; it was that some associations that they represented caused conflict for Sarah.

In addition to the anti-decorating I started working with the Risperdal dosage, not to exceed 4mg daily. By June 12, we noticed days of significant improvement and those coincided with using 1mg of Risperdal every four hours during the day. It did not mean that Sarah was completely at ease, she just seemed to be returning to her more normal state in bigger degrees and for longer durations. June was also turning to July. We checked the Lithium and it was at .6, not quite therapeutic. The doctor raised the dose of Lithium so that it could reach a therapeutic level.

I became so caught up in watching good patterns develop in school and at home, that we missed a Mayo genetics appointment on June 19; nevertheless the doctor sent along impressions from tests that had been started during Sarah's February stay. She mentioned normal MECP2 deletion/duplication analysis, which supplemented previously completed sequencing. The results from a skeletal survey did not show evidence of dysplasia or storage disease. A February 2006 EEG showed no evidence of seizures. (One doctor had wondered about eating epilepsy or seizure.) An MRI showed a small old lacunar infarct involving the right external capsule and right lateral basal ganglia region. She had normal blood ammonia and lactate levels, creatine kinase, liver enzymes, biotinidase, sterol panel, TSH, homocystine, and acylcarnitine profile, except for elevation of acetylcarnitine that could have been consistent with fasting, and normal urine mucopolysaccharides. No specific etiology for her condition had thus far been determined. Additional studies were considered, including comparative genomic hybridization array analysis, peroxisomal panel, co-enzyme Q, urine oligosaccharides, and urine acylglycines as well as a skin biopsy to look for chromosomal mosaicism, evidence of storage disease, and or for additional enzyme assays.

Ann Dunham

Sarah went back to school this morning. She was happy to go. Thursday through Sunday went good. Episodes were on board but we could work through it. When I went to school to give Sarah the 11:00 a.m. dose I was told she was having an excellent morning (Nurse still needed the order to administer Risperdal).

Date: 6/19/06
Behavior Cards

Time: 9:00–9:30 a.m.
Behavior: While asked to do something, she was already talking to herself and engaged in property destruction (1x), Screaming, Spitting (1x), Aggression (5x), Hitting (13x), Kicking (2x), and Throwing Object (7x).

Time: 9:30–10:00 a.m.
Behavior: An ongoing behavior was interrupted, and that resulted in property destruction (1x).

Time: 11:30 a.m.–12:00 p.m.
Behavior: When she could not get a desired item, she barked like a dog on her hands and knees (2x), Threw Items (4x) (This was during lunch).

Time: 12:30–1:00 p.m.
Behavior: During swimming, she was asked to do something that resulted in her getting out of the pool to push staff (1x), Grab Staff (15x), Hitting (20x), Kicking (20x), Property Dest. (2x), Stripping (5x), and some other stuff.

Time: 2:10 p.m.
Behavior: When asked to do something she screamed (3min), Spit (7x), Aggression (5x), Swore (7x).

Time: 3:00 p.m.
Behavior: When asked to do something she screamed (3min), Spit (15x).

Hello, Dr. Wells

I do wonder how much of this has continued for repertoire's sake. I am thinking it is slowly going to taper off to where she is not doing this stuff. I have been able to tell Sarah to stop these things and many times she does. I tell her in an informational way, without judgment. There have been a few times here and there where she has had a hard time and is not redirectable at home. But not near as bad as it was. The staff at school feels she is doing better than she was and seemed somewhat encouraged with how her day went. We went to the farm afterward and did all the normal stuff with the additional new thing of letting some ducklings out of their cage...

The next day's school incidents, while prevalent, were shorter in duration. During these particular days, Sarah started asking for a "tug", so that my encouragement and our combined wills could stave off the episodes. I was glad she asked for help. In late winter, I figured out that Sarah felt we were winning if she could be distracted from the episodes. One time, I softly tackled her upon a couch that she stood by, as she engaged in an episode. Immediately after I did that, she looked at me with amazement and said, "Good job Mom. We did it!" Another time, while she was in the unit I distracted her with a stuffed frog from the gift shop that made the "ribbit" noise. She had been engaged in an episode for quite some time when the frog distracted her. She looked over at me and said, "Yes," her eyes lighting up from a previously vacant stare and her face breaking into a smile. Those at the unit who had been alongside her, and quite worried, became pleased at the successful distraction; at that time, I think they feared malignant catatonia. With Sarah, the culmination of every experience seemed to be that of not quite knowing every element in the battle, but always trying anyway; the professionals who made a difference for Sarah represented such. The teachers were next in line to engage in the worthy battle. Sarah's wellness incrementally increased, usually signified by the degrees of her teachers' happiness. Happy teachers meant that all was right enough in her world. While there were still blips on the behavioral radar, the end of July signified celebration and a walk down memory lane.

Ann Dunham

(7/28/06) Hello Dr. Wells,
Sarah had a great Friday, even as the temperature soared
above 100 degrees. Staff at school is elated at how well she is
doing. I picked her up from school today; with the heat being
off the charts, I did not want her on a bus that did not have
air conditioning for the long ride. She has no behavior cards
today. Her language and ability to contribute to conversation is
wonderful. It was a year ago, on the last weekend of July, that
I had written about Sarah having to go to the emergency room
to get stitches because she hit the glass on the door at the farm.
That was due to internal conflict and her not being able to have
control during it. I had also mentioned that I was not sure what
to do about the meds and had just stopped Ativan. During that
time, she was also having trouble with sleeping at night. She is
doing much better now, on this 2006 last weekend in July! Even
when she has these slight episodes or internal things, she allows
for redirection and welcomes it. That concludes this walk down
memory lane.

In August, Sarah became better at trying to describe her challenges. One time, when she was obviously dealing with internal conflict of some sort, she told her father "Daddy I was dreaming," even though she had been awake the entire time. Steve then gave her a hug for comfort. Sarah had also started to seek other avenues of relief, as she only allowed for listening to the Christian music station in our area. She flatly rejected all the other stations programmed on the radio, and sang along to her only station's music. She talked about how "Jesus is God" and all I could think of was "From the mouths of babes." It is certainly conceivable that Sarah understands the singing of praises. Sarah described the character traits of the people she associated with who had joy, laughter, or smiling, and she indicated how they were like Jesus. She even flipped channels on the TV until she came across Christian programming. We did not consciously teach her these things.

෴

Hello, Dr. Wells

Sarah and the rest of us have uniquely learned about trusting God, one day at a time. My heart remains joyful as I consider her fruitful searching, especially given the fact that it started at about the same time in which I was reading in Jeremiah. "Call to me and I will answer you and tell you great and unsearchable things you do not know" (Verse 33:3). The Lord gave that word to Jeremiah and within context; there was the promise of eventual healing along with restoration for a land that was desolate. Sarah learned more than we expected and I believe it is because she earnestly sought a sustainable truth, her eternal comfort. Even in her hard times and struggles God continues to grow a faith in her; a faith in what has yet to be seen. We are not in His eternity yet, but we can believe in it from here.

The journey with our Sarah brought us to our refuge. Since we had been led to the land, we decided to live in it for real. As Jeff graduated from high school in 2007, we started the process of selling our place in the city and moving to our promise land. Jana, the middle child, remained tough and sacrificed her city life, even getting a couple of speeding tickets on the way since she became a commuter. As we took our steps toward the move to the country, Sarah continued to lean on her friend Jesus. An important aspect of her journey is that we made the move to reside in a place where she felt a sense of belonging; Sarah became able to achieve mighty things after that. First off, her classmates voted her Valentine's Queen for her day school's dance. More importantly, she showed sustained improvement while in the behavior room through the 2006/07 school year. Her teacher, Erin, then gently prodded me with the idea of transition to regular school. During the 2007/08 school year, Sarah started an incremental transition to a rather large high school with a PA system! It was a transition that I resisted but allowed. Her sister Jana attends the same high school, and Grandma Patsy is a lunch lady there. Having both there helped me to allow such a leap of faith. I did not want to see too much put upon Sarah, but I had to allow the possibilities on her horizon. On the first day of Sarah's transition to the high school, I looked at the case manager and quietly confided, "I don't think this is going to work";

that comment indicating that my faith was not yet complete. I was wrong about if things would work, but only because the teachers and aides represented friends on Sarah's horizon, willing to practice much more grace then I expected. In so doing, they have walked through all her differing seasons. They even were able to see some of her actual baseline, what I like to call her summer! Sarah's high school experience is for another book, as she has many seasons to go before her next transition to life after school. Uncle Wayne sees "Sarah's Organic Produce" as a possibility, but we will not know for a few years yet.

〰️

Throughout the troubling times, a doctor has greatly endeared himself to us. My husband will have the last word, and that will be quite a surprise for him. Perhaps Steve can write the next book. Here is his note of thanks to Dr. Wells.

Dear Dr. Wells,
I cannot tell you the countless times I have sat and begun to write this letter. Even now, I find that there are no words that can adequately express my sincere gratitude and thankfulness for what you have meant to us over the years. I know that you have extended an open arm for us that reaches far beyond your profession. This is just one reason we hold you so dearly and know that you are a blessing from the Lord. As you know we have had our challenges, as many do in this life. Our family has seen its share of adversity, none more so than our Sarah. We accepted the many challenges, even when we did not know how we were going to do it. (Just accepting our calling.) One thing that enabled us to carry on was your unwavering determination to help us. When so many others seem to just give up, you never did. As long as we were willing to carry on, so were you. This gave us great hope and great determination to care for Sarah. Our love for her reaches to our very soul and defines who we are. More specifically it expresses our unconditional love, just as we believe the Lord has this same kind of love for us. We have experienced some pretty miraculous

things over the past several years since this all came about. One of those miracles we believe was finding yourself and the staff there at Mayo. If you can impart anything to those you may mentor, compassion to walk along side those who need it most.
Forever Grateful, Steve

Ann Dunham

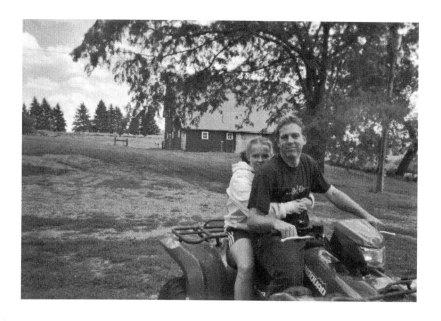

Steve and Sarah on quad

Hello, Dr. Wells

Jeff and Jana!

Yell!
I'll try not to yell.
Keep wishing me well.
Makes me ten times as old,
when all I do is scold.
Don't do this, don't do that,
I'm an old bat.
I'm a major dope,
when at the end of my rope.
My kids aren't pests.
I just need more rest.
When they whine,
a hug they must find.
Everything need not be in place,
just the smiles on their faces.
Need more smiles and love.
Get strength from above!
(Written one night in 1993, after yelling too much during the day.)

Ann Dunham

Jana's Feet

Feet in my hair.
I will not despair.
It's Jana…
She is at it again.
The middle friend.
She's between the other two.
What do you mean whom?
She puts up with them every day,
it's Jeff and Sarah who are in her way.
Seems to me the middle one
has to shine brighter than the sun.
She's not the first or last,
so sometimes she gets passed.
One minute she's dependent,
then someone is the defendant.
So remember,
it's Jana whose the boss.
It's her you don't cross.
Jana's feet in my hair,
guess they can stay there.
(Written on day in 1993, after taking a nap with Jana)

Hello, Dr. Wells

Jeffrey

Hey little guy,
always asking why.
Is there anything you won't try?
Everything catches your eye,
even the smallest alibi.
You know a lie,
and again ask why.
Little fart.
You think you're so smart.
Trouble is, you are.
That much I've seen so far.
Since you're so smart,
could you master the art
…of whispering.
Maybe we could softly sing,
or something equally satisfying.
We could try something quiet,
not loud.
Of you, I'd still be proud,
even without the attention of the crowd.

Ann Dunham

Jeff

Little Man
Weight of the world
on his little shoulders.
What will life hold for him,
as he gets older?
Will convictions become weak,
or much bolder?
Will his smile wear thin,
as the years do him in?
What type of witness
am I setting for him?
Life's many secrets,
where to begin?
The uphill battle,
I pray he will win.

Hello, Dr. Wells

Steve

Inspiration Basketball

A look of purpose
shining in his eyes.
Catching a rebound,
as if he could fly.
Found his home,
on wooden floors with ten foot rims.
I could imagine
something special in him.
Not his hair or height,
nor his strength and might.
Just an ageless demeanor,
noble and earnest.
No such worry,
will he win or lose?
Just the game in fluid motion,
team given ceaseless devotion.

Set apart for this time,
what do I find?
For him the game and living life,
are very much the same.

☙

3368494

Made in the USA